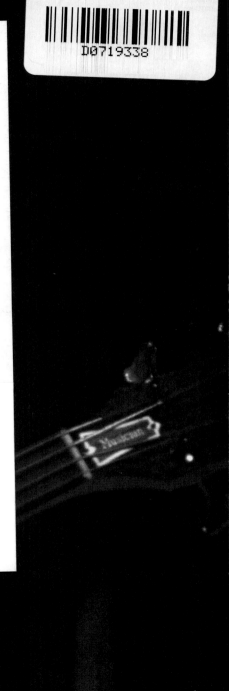

412

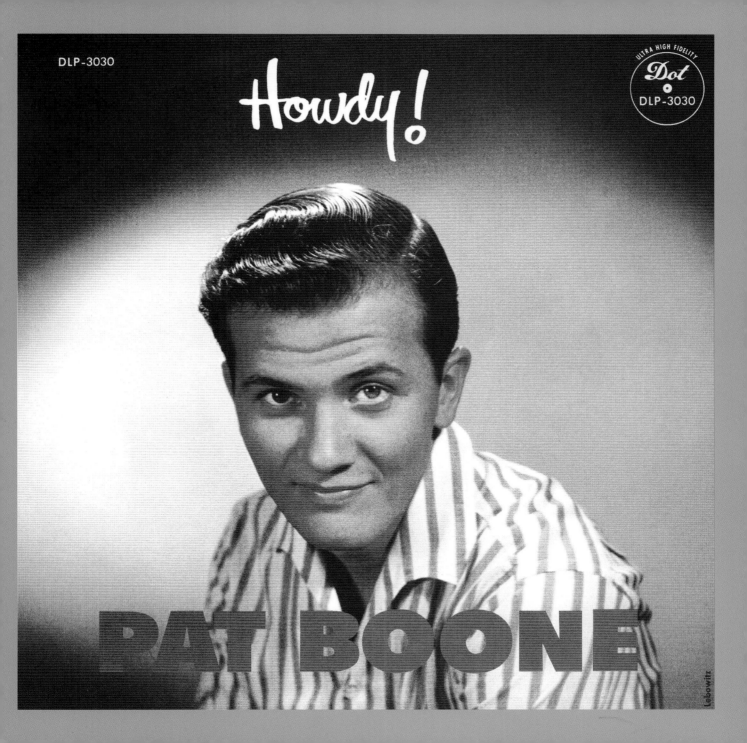

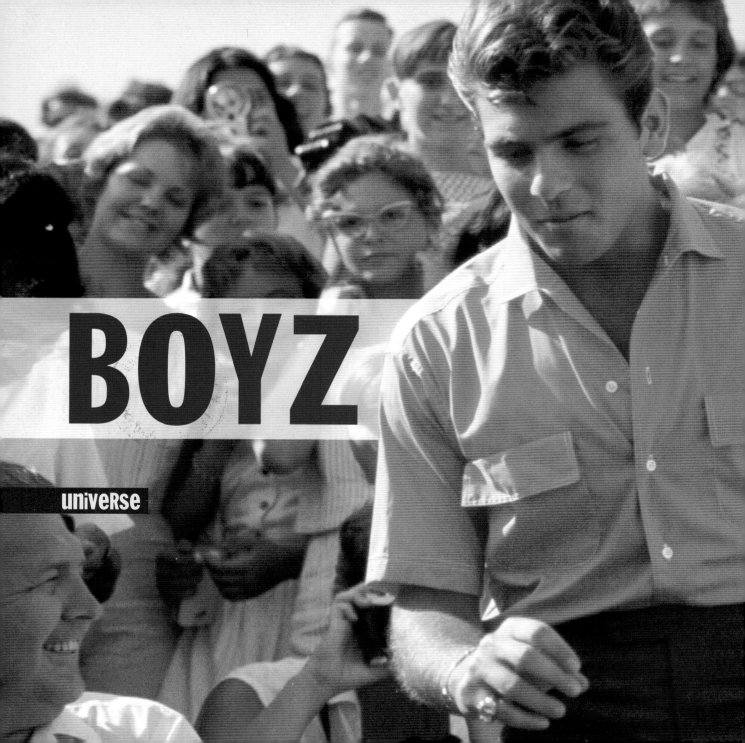

and THe **BANDZ**

THE HOTTEST MEN in MUSiC: From ELViS TO *NSYNC

DonaLD f. ReuTer

First published in the United States of America in 2002 by
UNIVERSE PUBLISHING
A Division of Rizzoli International Publications, Inc.
300 Park Avenue South
New York, NY 10010

Designed by
Donald F. Reuter

Printed in Hong Kong

2002 2003 2004
2005 2006 2007
10 9 8 7 6 5 4 3 2 1

Library of Congress Control
Number: 2001099805

on the cover, from top left
to right: Jeff Timmons
(see page 5), Bryan
Adams (142), David Bowie
(10), Shaun Cassidy (83),
Michael Jackson (85),
Jim Morrison (118), Jon
Bon Jovi (148), Bono
(150), Kevin Richardson
(102), Bryan Abrams (100),
Kurt Cobain (122), Harry
Connick Jr. (152), David Soul
(38), Scott Stapp (114), Billy Ray
Cyrus (61), Michael Damian (40),
Simon LeBon (97), Enrique Iglesias
(47), Jaron Lowenstein (57), Fred
Durst (130), Garth Brooks (65),
Roger Daltrey (138), Mark McGrath
(155), Morten Harket (49),
Joshua Scott "J.C." Chasez (9),
Bobby Sherman (81), Darren
Hayes (56), Martin Kemp (96),
Robbie Williams (101), and Mark
Wahlberg (43).

STING

front endpaper: (b. Gordon Matthew Sumner, 10/2/51, Wallsend, England) The eldest of four children, Sumner was in a half dozen bands before he partnered with Stewart Copeland and Andy Summers to form the highly influential eighties rock band, The Police. Before he turned musician, Sting worked as a ditch digger, English schoolteacher, and soccer coach. His devotion to the latter sport inspired his nickname; he was called Sting (originally Stinger) for wearing a yellow-and-black striped soccer sweater. (I bet he looked damned good in it too!) Sting is a multi-talented instrumentalist (he plays a num-ber of guitars, the piano, harmonica, mandolin, saxophone, and flute), and his composition "Every Breath You Take" was The Police's biggest hit. Despite belief to the contrary, it was not a love song, but rather the ruminations of a man stalking an ex-girlfriend. Yikes! Such surprisingly written works became Sting's hallmark, as a group member *and* soloist. Two years before the band broke up (on a high note with *Synchronicity*), this *bee*-utiful boy was already on the fast track to a successful second career; by the time of his seventh album, the hypnotic and spell-binding *Brand New Day* (his bestseller), he had firmly established himself as a leading music force—and physical evidence that some men do indeed age quite well! (Denis O'Regan/Corbis)

opening page: Pat Boone, on the cover of his second album, *Howdy!*, released by Dot in 1956. (author's collection)

title page: Teen sensation Fabian, performing at a 1960 outdoor concert. For more on this "prince" among teen idols, see page 77. (Corbis)

EDDIE FISHER

left (b. Edwin John Fisher, 8/10/28, Philadelphia, Pa.) In the late fifties, when Fisher left his then-wife, popular actress Debbie Reynolds, to be with her good friend and fellow thespian Elizabeth Taylor, the resulting *scandale* became world news. His adulterous behavior quickly overshadowed his hugely successful singing ("Any Time" and "Oh, My Papa") and budding acting career. However, on some level this philandering only enhanced the social (and sexu-al) status of the one time protégé of stage and screen star Eddie Cantor; it also reinforced the notion that all popular male singers were irresistible to beautiful women. Nevertheless, Fisher's subsequent marriage to Taylor did not last, nor did the one that followed to starlet Connie Stevens. Oh well, *que sera, sera!* Fisher is father to actress/author Carrie Fisher and actress Joely Fisher. He is also the winner of a 1958 Golden Globe for Best TV Show, for *Coke Time.* (Everett)

This book is dedicated to all the girls *and* boys (women *and* men) who ever spent a single moment swooning (and sweating) over the sound (and sight) of a "hot" man on the microphone. *Boyz* is for you.

98 DEGREES

clockwise, from top left: Justin Jeffré (2/25/73, Mount Clemens, Mich.), (An)drew Lachey (8/8/76, Cincinnati, Ohio), Nick Lachey (11/9/73, Harlan, Ky.), and Jeff Timmons (4/30/73, Canton, Ohio) If your attraction to male-dominant musical groups is, for whatever reason, purely salacious, then for a surefire shot to your libido look no further than this *hottest*—and by that I mean bodily—of boy bands. (However, categorizing them as a "band" is unfair; professionally they far more resemble turn-of-the-century barbershop quartets and male vocal groups of the forties and fifties.) Timmons, a onetime Kent State University student and acting hopeful, first teamed up with Nick Lachey, an avid sports enthusiast in Los Angeles. They were joined by Jeffré, a former classmate and performing partner of Lachey's in Cincinnati, and eventually by Lachey's younger brother Drew. With the foursome set, they took their tight harmonies (and biceps) into the densely populated teen market to make a dent. Now, if one could just get past the fact that Jeff, Nick, and Drew—sorry Justin!—have the most near-perfect bodies you could ever hope to see, one might realize that their hits, like "Give Me Just One Night," are just as much worth a listen as the group is worth a look. (All Action/Retna)

contentz

opposite: (b. 5/31/62, Montreal, Canada) Anyone audacious enough to wear "shades" during the evening owes a debt of thanks to this dude and his hit debut single, aptly titled, "Sunglasses at Night." The youngest of five children raised in Spain, Mexico, and Florida, Hart wanted to be a singer for as long as he could remember and was aided in the beginning by some rather substantial talent: a chance meeting with Tom Jones led to an introduction to fellow Canadian singer Paul Anka. The legendary singer was so impressed by the then-thirteen-year-old's skills that he financed Hart's earliest recordings. Unfortunately, none of these releases had much of an impact. Many years would pass before he laid the track for "Sunglasses" and became an overnight sensation. Now just past forty and well beyond teenybopper status, what is a former teen idol to do who is still attractive (possibly more so) and still talented? For Hart, that meant a turn to adult contemporary music and the release of his eighth (and counting) self-produced album. The guy will "never surrender." (Everett)

this page: (b. Robert Ridarelli, 2/26/42, Philadelphia, Pa.) When Dick Clark's

BOBBY rYDELL

Philadelphia-based show *American Bandstand* became must-see television in the late fifties, the city itself became a hotbed of musical talent. Literally thousands of anxious idols-to-be from the town of "brotherly love" popped up, including Fabian and Frankie Avalon, but Rydell, a gifted drummer, singer, and actor (*Bye, Bye, Birdie*, 1963) was a standout personality. For a few short years, he and his signature pompadour hairstyle were seen and heard everywhere, and audiences were driven to near-hysterics wherever he went. But fads change and fans move on. When the British boy-bands (Beatles, Searchers, etc.) hit our shores in the mid-sixties, Rydell and his comely cohorts proved no match for the massing "mop tops." However, Rydell's undeniable and enduring popularity is so indicative of that bygone and beloved period, producers of the infinitely popular musical *Grease* named their high school setting in his honor. (Corbis)

SiNG, BOY, SiNG!

Nowhere is the often up-and-down, roller-coaster dynamic of popular culture more apparent than within the confines of recorded music—more specifically, in the category of pop music. There, a consumer's momentary (and long term) interests *drive* the industry, and nothing will get the petal to the metal faster than a signpost up ahead emblazoned with the face of a handsome man. *Nothing*. To the diligent (even casual) observer, this interchange has given us years of (guilty) pleasure by jamming the highways to success—and back—with an abundance of gorgeous guys, whom, unless you were stalled at the starting line, you could not help but notice. It has certainly enlivened life's journey with a pleasant diversion or two (and, at the very least, led this author to do *Boyz and the Bandz*).

This book is not really about per se boys (very few, actually), bands (only a small percentage could claim instrumentalist as a main profession), or even boy-bands (as you may have suspected). It is simply a glossy photographic tribute to *all* walks of men in music, who just happened to be—by some very lucky twist of fate—as famous for their fabulous faces (sometimes bodies) as for their music.

This criteria made it relatively easy to determine whose gazes should grace its pages: good-looking male singers. But, not every one is included. As would be the case, there are limits on time, space, and money. There is also the simple fact that not

TOMMY SANDS (b. 8/27/37, Chicago, Ill.) As a recording artist,

Sands was a rather perfunctory instrumentalist (who learned to play the guitar at age seven) and singer. However, in the looks category he was never anything less than primo, the perfect mold to be cast as a teen idol. From the start, this gorgeous guy was given all the right chances—but had his share of bad luck. Colonel Tom Parker of Eddy Arnold and Elvis Presley fame was an early mentor, but Sands's freshman efforts failed. Even when his fame rivaled that of Elvis, which it did during Sands's most successful year, 1957, his "hits" were relatively inconsequential (do you remember "Teen-Age Crush"?). With such a pretty puss, it was a no-brainer that Sands would become a movie "star"; his first film was as the lead in the quasi-autobiographical musical *Sing, Boy, Sing*. But he was never much more than set decoration. For five years, sexy-boy was also married to Nancy Sinatra, daughter of Frank. But after their divorce, it was said that father dearest did everything he could to sideline his ex-son-in-law's career. Ultimately, Sands may have been too handsome for his own good, and as the decades passed, any legitimate contributions he may have made to music were covered over by talk of his cover-boy appearance. (Corbis)

*nsync *clockwise, from top left:* Justin Timberlake (b. 1/31/81, Memphis, Tenn.), Lancton "Lance" Bass (b. 5/4/79, Clinton, Miss.), Chris Kirkpatrick (b. 10/17/71, Pittsburgh), Joshua Scott "JC" Chasez (b. 8/8/76, Washington, D.C.), and Joey Fatone (b. 1/28/77, New York City) Formed in Orlando, Florida, this quintet surpassed the popularity of their arch rivals, Backstreet Boys, when they released the 2000 album *No Strings Attached* and it became the fastest selling CD of all time—two million copies in one week! They went on to receive the ultimate accolade when *Rolling Stone* dubbed them "the biggest band in the world." As youngsters, members Timberlake and Chasez both appeared on Disney's "Mickey Mouse Club" (a revolving cast that also included Christina Aguilera and Britney Spears, Timberlake's main squeeze), before being corralled into the famed group by former New Kids on the Block management in 1995. (Note: Timberlake's mother came up with the name *NSYNC by combining the last letters of each member's first names—*clever* woman!) (Bob Berg/Retna)

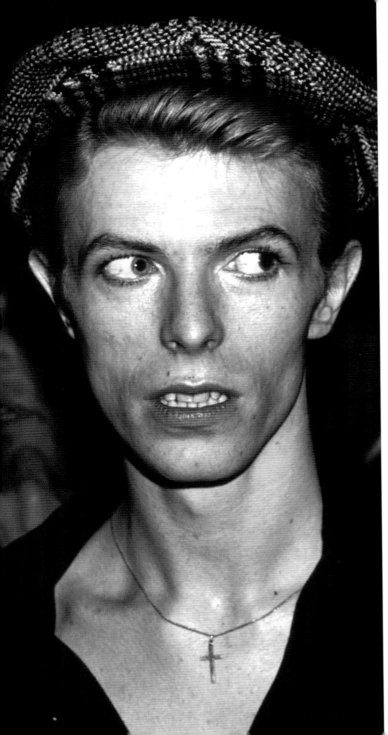

all male singers became popular, *even slightly*, due to their physical appearance. Therefore (and this is not a judgment of looks), you will not see some extremely well-liked male talent.

Boyz is also a bit of a dual cultural history lesson. (Don't worry, certainly nothing heavy—and it's filled with pictures!) The first part shows that for all the "news" created by the latest wave of bright-smiled, buff-bodied beauties—which some say first moved toward us in the late eighties with New Edition and New Kids on the Block and *ended* with double aught acts like O-Town and Aaron Carter (brother of Backstreet Boy Nick Carter)—the "phenomena" has happened many, many times before (and it will not be the last). The second part shows how tastes in men have grown—not necessarily *advanced*—over the course of roughly a century. (Note that the first appearance of the "true" teen idol is generally agreed to be the mid-fifties.) Who among us would list a brow-tweezed Rudy Vallee or a snip-nosed Bing Crosby as a "hot" male singer today, even though it is quite obvious in their heyday they were all the rage? Conversely, would any of our grandparents mention a Fred Durst or Eminem in the same breath when speaking of blissful talents like Frank Sinatra, even Fabian? Not likely. You may even find yourself wondering "What was I thinking?" at the same time you ponder "I never thought of him."

Last, *Boyz* is a slight commentary on the transitory nature of stardom. Beyond looks, most of the men share this suitably "dramatized" career path: anonymous talented youth is discovered and marked for stardom; he is groomed (bodily and mentally) and placed in the market to maximize potential; material is released, first singles, then an album, exceeding sales expectations, and a superstar is born "overnight" (regardless of whether he has worked since childhood); his name appears in the "in" column of a well-read entertainment magazine; sophomore product is hastily thrown together, but still sells; the most troublesome sign that the "boy" has arrived, a flood of copycat artists (some more beautiful than the original); riffs appear between talent and management, causing behind-the-scenes changes; the much-anticipated junior album is released, with all eyes on the chart; despite some of his "best work," sales are *way* down; a scramble ensues to place blame; a fourth album is planned, recorded, shelved; name appears in the "out" column of a well-read entertainment magazine. Our fine fellow has gone from zero to one hundred and back—almost to where he started—in less than a few years. His audience has placed him on the shelf with the rest and moved on to the next boy. Addendum: a few years down the road, redressed, our man jumps into the current market. A valiant attempt to rekindle his stalled career, the bid is unsuccessful. Reasoning: his appearance smacks of desperation; he is perceived as out of place and worse, too old, for present audience tastes. Transpose this template over the career patterns of many in *Boyz*, and it will fit perfectly. But enough of moribund thoughts.

Surely, he (and his group) may not last forever. They may also look different, wear different clothes, twist their hips to a different beat from those who have come before—and after. But ultimately, though the faces may change, the sentiment remains the same for the time being: if he's hot, he's happening. For our purposes, that's all that matters.

DaViD BOWie

opposite: (b. David Robert Jones, 1/8/47, London) As a young man, the "chameleon of pop" tried unsuccessfully to work as a commercial artist, before deciding the right career choice would be something in music. In the beginning, he used a sweetened version of his own name, Davie Jones, but changed it when it became a conflict with a London stage actor (and soon-to-be Monkee) Davy Jones. Musically inspired by jazz and a student of mime (to some fans, that would be rather obvious), boney Bowie progressed very slowly upward. *Very.* Finally in 1969, after viewing the film *2001: A Space Odyssey*, he wrote "Space Oddity," his fictional tale of "Major Tom." The single rocketed Bowie out of the obscure *mod* ranks. In 1972, he debuted his "Ziggy Stardust" incarnation—simultaneously confessing to the press his bisexuality. His audacity, both physical and spiritual, threatened to overshadow the neophyte star's burgeoning talent. Undeterred, he scored his first number-one song, "Fame" (cowritten by John Lennon) in 1975. A short time after, the now "Thin White Duke" became a rather unique film actor—well-suited to unusual parts, such as his roles in *The Man Who Fell to Earth* (playing an alien) and *The Hunger* (as a vampire). During the late seventies, drugs and health problems kept him to the sidelines, but his Brian Eno—produced album, *Scary Monsters* (1980) is considered his finest work. His biggest hit came via dancemeister Nile Rodgers of Chic with the release of "Let's Dance" (1983), and Bowie was looking surprisingly handsome, with a new short coiff and pearl gray suit. Singing star as cultural icon, groundbreaker, and husband to supermodel Iman, the "guy with the different colored eyes" (the result of a childhood fight injury) is the wealthiest rock star in the United Kingdom: a testament not only to his popularity and wise investments, but remarkable longevity as well. (Michael Ochs)

this page: (b. 1/24/41, Brooklyn) This boy from Brooklyn (who attended the # neiL DiamonD
same high school as singer-songwriter Neil Sedaka) has enjoyed great success as a musical storyteller and master of the mid-tempo ballad for nearly four decades. Diamond began his musical career at age sixteen and attended New York University as a premed student (on a fencing scholarship, no less!) before working his way through the halls of New York's infamous Brill Building (a haven for the most gifted songwriting talent in the late fifties and sixties), then emerging as a world-class artist with "Cracklin' Rosie," "Sweet Caroline," "Song Sung Blue," and "I'm a Believer" (a hit for The Monkees), among many other familiar tunes. Surprisingly, his 1978 duet with Barbra Streisand, "You Don't Bring Me Flowers," came about purely by accident: a savvy radio disc jockey spliced together two solo tracks recorded by each artist. Realizing the potential, the two performers quickly entered the studio together and laid down the track that was to become Diamond's biggest hit. Often presenting himself as a dark-haired, denim- and leather-clad urbanite, with a penchant for country-folk-tinged music, Diamond was loved by women for his brooding demeanor. Today, a touch less melancholy, he still retains his sullen charm and a sizeable audience. (Harry Goodwin/Michael Ochs)

rudy vallee

this page: (b. Hubert Prior Vallee, 7/28/01, Island Pond, Vt., d. 7/3/86)

Dressed in a raccoon coat topped off with a panama hat, Vallee, megaphone in hand, was the penultimate 1920s collegiate cheerleader. Though initially not thought of as much of a singer, he fronted one of the most successful big bands of the age ("Brother, Can You Spare a Dime?"), and with a "heigh-ho, everybody" as his famous call, Vallee and troupe became one of early radio's greatest and most popular acts. In his day, Vallee personally attracted much of the same fan adulation we have become accustomed to seeing today—although with his manicured brows and downturned eyelids (enhanced with shadow) he would appear rather too dandy-fied by modern standards. When movies replaced radio as the favorite form of mass entertainment, Vallee continued his success. Originally cast in romantic leads, he segued into character parts, playing off his pompous, New England demeanor. His most notable acting role was that of J. B. Biggley, in the 1961 Pulitzer Prize—winning musical *How to Succeed in Business without Really Trying,* which he reprised in the 1967 film version. (Everett)

arTie sHaw

opposite: (b. Arthur Jacob Arshawsky, 5/23/10, New York City) As a young teen, Shaw was a gifted saxophone and clarinet player (his favorite instrument) and showed great promise as a music arranger and director. When he formed his own band in 1937, it was a resounding success. Surprisingly, the man who brought us the hit "Begin the Beguine," among others was not fond of publicity and fame, but his notoriety and good looks thwarted any plans he may have had for anonymity; Shaw was, to put it bluntly, the "cat's meow" to his millions of female fans. Yet his dislike of public attention is somewhat at odds with his actions: this lyrical Lothario had eight wives, among them two of filmdom's reigning sex symbols—Ava Gardner and Lana Turner. Aside from his private exploits, perhaps a more appropriate way to remember Shaw's legacy is his then-radical color-blind attitude toward hiring policies: among other black musicians with whom he included on the payroll was the legendary Billie Holiday. (Michael Ochs)

LeaDerz OF THe BanDz

BiNG CrOSBY

this page: (b. Harry Lillis Crosby, 5/3/03, Tacoma, Wash., d. 10/14/77) A typical "crooner" is defined as a man who sings in a soft, gentle, and sentimental manner. This is exactly the way Crosby sang, and since he was, arguably, the first "pop" music idol he became the archetype of these melodious fellows. Prior to his arriving on the music scene in the late-twenties, the recording industry was still going through the throes of adolescence. Fortunately, by the time Crosby released his first solo hits in 1931 (including "Just One More Chance") three very important things had come into their own: advanced recording technology, radio, and musical film. Their timely appearance all but guaranteed his success. Although his musical style did not please everyone, he became the most popular artist of the first half of the twentieth century. When all was said and done, Crosby amassed an astounding three-hundred-plus(!) Top 40 hits, over thirty number-one songs, the best-selling *single* recording of all time—the wartime holiday classic "White Christmas" (until it was replaced by Elton John's tribute to Princess Diana "Candle in the Wind" in 1997)—an Oscar (for Best Actor of 1944, in *Going My Way*), and other important awards too numerous to mention. His vast popularity is notable given the fact that he was rather average looking (proof that handsomeness is not absolutely necessary for success), hardly a strong singer, and was said to be, on the personal side, rather nasty and abusive. (Photofest)

opposite: (b. Francis Albert Sinatra, 12/12/15, Hoboken, N.J., d. 5/15/98) Many music critics, historians, and fans consider this man *the* greatest popular singer of the twentieth century—ahead of Bing Crosby, Elvis, and the Beatles! Skinny Frank began his life very poor, singing in bars before finding work with bandleader Harry James, then Tommy Dorsey. His physical frailty and caressingly soft voice ("I'll Never Smile Again") made him appear and sound nonthreateningly romantic—still a potent combination for success today—and the object of affection for millions of bobby-soxers. During the forties, he also entered into filmmaking and made the most of limited acting ability, culminating in a supporting actor Oscar win for the wartime classic *From Here to Eternity* (1953). (Note: Sinatra did not serve in the armed forces due to an ear injury sustained in his youth.) Beginning in the 1950s, when he was no longer the darling of the teen set, Sinatra began a new musical journey (with Capitol Records) and recorded many of his most popular works—beginning with "Young at Heart" (1954), through to "Strangers in the Night" (1966). Collaborating with gifted arranger Nelson Riddle, among many others, this extended, lightly jazz-influenced period is considered his "golden age" and resulted in many of the most exquisitely produced and important pieces in the history of recorded music. (Everett)

FranK sinaTra

of THe PacK

Harry Belafonte

this page: (b. 3/1/27, Harlem, N.Y.) Though black men (and women) played an integral part in the diversity and cultural integrity of the recording industry since its inception, their contributions and presence were largely underplayed. To say the least, by the fifties it was time to start making amends. Beginning in the early part of the decade, Belafonte (who was raised in Jamaica by his mother) took his unique repertoire of folk and calypso songs and became a nationwide sensation. Subsequently, he, along with Sammy Davis Jr., broke through the longstanding racial barriers that had limited the ascent of ethnic entertainers. Belafonte's rise was also noteworthy because during a time of arch conservativism he had a palpably sexual presence; he was quite stunning to look at—frequently described as "beautiful"—and often dressed to show off a fantastic body. Within ten years of his arrival, Belafonte had won a 1953 Tony award for *John Murray Anderson's Almanac*, had a number-one hit "Banana Boat Song (Day-O)," sold millions of records, became the first black performer to win an Emmy award (in 1960, for his variety special *Tonight with Belafonte*)—and forever changed the "face" of popular music. (Bettmann/Corbis)

opposite: (b. Pierino Roland Como, 5/18/12, Canonsburg, Pa., d. 5/12/01) Stylistically, Como had a vocal sound similar to Bing Crosby, but his delivery was even more extreme: he sang with a hesitancy that bordered on the lethargic (once shamelessly parodied by the infamous SCTV comedy troupe). Regardless, his manner was so endearing that he became one of the top-selling recording artists of all time—charting through five decades—and performed live into his mid-eighties. Como worked as a barber when he was a young man but left home to pursue a music career after graduating high school. He joined the Ted Weems Orchestra in 1937, and lasted with them until their breakup in the early forties. Moving back to Pennsylvania, he picked up his hair clippers again but was tracked down and signed to headline his own weekly radio show on CBS and a recording contract with RCA. Over the years, he stacked up an impressive amount of Top 10 hits, ranging from "Til the End of Time" (based on Chopin's Polonaise in A-Flat Minor) and "Papa Loves Mambo" to "It's Impossible." His recording of "Catch a Falling Star" was also the first RIAA certified gold record. Como became a leading television star as well; his variety show was a consistent high rater and is an outstanding example of the genre. (One contract for his services was, at twenty-five million dollars, the largest sum ever paid to a television entertainer at the time.) Seated atop a stool or on the sofa of his "living room," dressed in his all-too-familiar cardigan or pullover sweater (and looking eerily like President George W. Bush!), Como introduced the singing talent of hundreds to millions of viewers, forever casting himself as music's Mr. Nice Guy (he was also called "Mr. Christmas"), and won two Emmy awards for his benevolence. (Michael Ochs)

perry como

easY DuZ iT

TONY BENNETT

(b. Anthony Dominick Benedetto, 8/13/26, Astoria, Queens, N.Y.) A grocer's son, Bennett first found "work" as a singer with the entertainment division of the United States Army in World War II. After his enlistment ended he went to work in New York City, performing at a variety of clubs—including a stint for Pearl Bailey—under the name of Joe Bari. Bennett's career took off when he was "discovered" by Bob Hope, who recommended a name change and asked him to perform in the comedian's show at the Paramount Theatre. In 1950 he signed with Columbia Records and released "Because of You" in 1951, which became the biggest song of the year. Many hits followed, including "Rags to Riches" and "Stranger in Paradise," but his signature song will always be "I Left My Heart in San Francisco," which won the Grammy for Record of the Year in 1962. Bennett has enjoyed success far longer than many of his peers by wisely recording with contemporary artists—his *MTV Unplugged* album won him the Grammy for Album of the Year in 1995. Bennett also studied fine art and is a well-regarded painter. (MPTV)

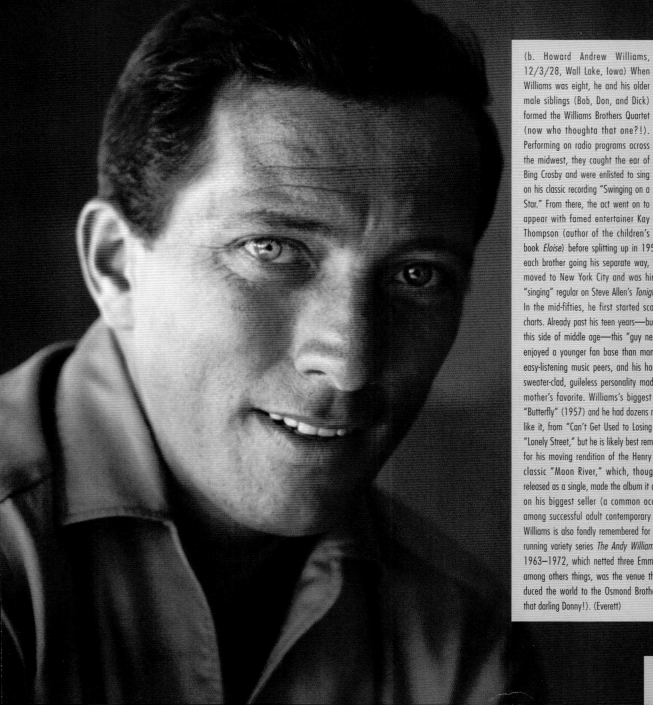

(b. Howard Andrew Williams, 12/3/28, Wall Lake, Iowa) When Williams was eight, he and his older male siblings (Bob, Don, and Dick) formed the Williams Brothers Quartet (now who thoughta that one?!). Performing on radio programs across the midwest, they caught the ear of Bing Crosby and were enlisted to sing on his classic recording "Swinging on a Star." From there, the act went on to appear with famed entertainer Kay Thompson (author of the children's book *Eloise*) before splitting up in 1951. With each brother going his separate way, Williams moved to New York City and was hired as a "singing" regular on Steve Allen's *Tonight Show*. In the mid-fifties, he first started scaling the charts. Already past his teen years—but *well* to this side of middle age—this "guy next door" enjoyed a younger fan base than many of his easy-listening music peers, and his homespun, sweater-clad, guileless personality made him a mother's favorite. Williams's biggest hit was "Butterfly" (1957) and he had dozens more just like it, from "Can't Get Used to Losing You" to "Lonely Street," but he is likely best remembered for his moving rendition of the Henry Mancini classic "Moon River," which, though never released as a single, made the album it appeared on his biggest seller (a common occurrence among successful adult contemporary artists). Williams is also fondly remembered for his long-running variety series *The Andy Williams Show*, 1963–1972, which netted three Emmys, and, among others things, was the venue that introduced the world to the Osmond Brothers (and that darling Donny!). (Everett)

JOHNNY MATHIS

opposite: (b. John Royce Mathis, 9/30/35, Gilmer, Tex.) The fourth of seven children, young John enjoyed singing for dad—whom he considered his best friend. It was apparent from the start that little John possessed a beautiful singing voice, but Mathis was a skilled track and field athlete as well. When he had to decide between the two paths in life, he was understandably traumatized. The world knows what course he chose—and his selection of a music career could not have been timed more perfectly. Thanks to inroads made by Harry Belafonte and Sammy Davis Jr., the general public was now more accepting of black entertainers—certainly more so than they had been a few short years before—and Mathis's introduction into the world of entertainment took full advantage of the situation. Mathis was discovered by an executive of Columbia Records, when Mathis was appearing in a San Francisco club. The savvy gentleman cabled his company with this famous note: "Have found a phenomenal 19 year old boy who could go all the way. Send blank contracts." Marketed as a "boy next door" type, his nonaggressive yet sensualized persona enabled Mathis to be embraced by an even larger audience than that of his predecessors. To say that he enjoyed spectacular success is an understatement: his first compilation album, *Johnny's Greatest Hits* (1958) stayed on the charts for over eight years! However, one should not assume that the man who gave us "Chances Are" and "Misty" enjoyed the fruits of his labors without hardship; even at the peak of his popularity he still had to contend with racism and hatred from individuals frightened by his unhindered rise to fame. (Corbis)

LETTERMEN

this page, from left to right: Bob Engemann (2/19/36, Highland Park, Mich.), Jim Pike (11/6/38, St. Louis, Mo.), Tony Butula (11/20/40, Sharon, Penn.) If two heads are better than one, then how about three? This bit of logic certainly paid off when Brigham Young University "letterman" Pike joined forces with fellow student Engemann and supper club singer Butala in the early sixties. The novel threesome took their pleasant harmonies and collegiate swagger straight to the top of adult contemporary playlists; wholesome and slow-tempoed compared to the ever-popular "beat" groups (The Beatles, Beach Boys, etc.) they were a tad less successful on mainstream pop charts. Nevertheless, this was an intentional musical choice, and it allowed them to flourish on the nightclub circuit and in small venues, continuing to this day, though their lineup has gone through many changes. Among their many hits, The Lettermen can include at least one truly classic recording: "Goin' Out of My Head/Can't Take My Eyes Off of You" (1967), which is a splendid example of their work and a unique two-hit medley. (Photofest)

21

BOBBY VINTON

(b. Stanley Robert Vinton, 4/16/35, Canonsburg, Pa.) While still in high school, Vinton formed his own band and was signed to a label, but numerous releases failed to find significant buyers. As a last ditch effort to keep his career afloat, it was decided that Vinton would be featured as a soloist on the next offering. Though he never considered his voice noteworthy, the effort paid off. The single, "Roses Are Red (My Love)" (1962) was a super smash. Surprisingly, he continued to chart when the British invasion all but dominated the popular music scene: one of his biggest singles, "There! I've Said It Again!," was the last number-one pop song before the Beatles replaced it with "I Wanna Hold Your Hand"—and changed music forever. For a time "The Polish Prince" fell out of favor, but his career was resuscitated twice: in the mid-seventies, with the quirky, polka-esque hit, "My Melody of Love" (which has the distinction of being the only American pop hit sung partially in Polish); and when director David Lynch used his hit version of "Blue Velvet" in the disturbing film of the same name. It has since become his most requested song. (Michael Ochs)

22

(b. John Allan Jones, 1/14/38, Los Angeles, Calif.) Dreamboat Jack inherited his good looks from an actress mother, Irene Hervey, and actor/singer father, Allan Jones. As a young man, he joined dad's nightclub act, but soon grew restless and left to pursue a solo career. Originally, record executives wanted to take their latest charge and turn him into a rock teen idol, but Jones scoffed at the idea. He preferred the more soothing sounds of ballads and standards. Eventually becoming one of the top male singers of the sixties (and early seventies), Jones was successful with a number of songs, including two—"Lollipops and Roses" (1962) and "Wives and Lovers" (1964)—which both won Grammys for Best Pop Performance by a Male. Regrettably, he may be best remembered for his singing of the kitschy seventies theme song for TV's *Love Boat*. (Yeech!) Like many of his cohorts— Andy Williams, Bobby Vinton, Johnny Mathis, et al—Jones was notably attractive, abundantly talented, and relatively young. But, as was the case with his fellow crooners, he and his work mainly appealed to an older audience. While the pop market continued to distinguish itself with music geared largely for teens, Jones's followers found themselves placed into their own separate niche market: adult contemporary. To verify its importance, *Billboard* magazine gave the category its own chart, first under the name "Easy Listening" in 1961. Interestingly, this mature group gravitated toward buying albums—not singles—because the long play factor of a 33rpm record worked well with the accompanying AC lifestyle; a continual stream of music was key to the success of a chic, "grown-up only" cocktail party or romantic dinner. No breaks in melody to spoil the mood! (Photofest)

JACK JONES

MUSIC MaESTRO, PLeez!

opposite: (b. 4/10/10, Cambridge, Mass., d. 2/9/51) If someone as famously attractive as actor Tyrone Power is chosen to portray you on film (*The Eddy Duchin Story*, 1956), is there any doubt what effect you must have had on fans? Undeniably sexy (at times, stunningly so) with a marvelous head full of longish, wavy brown hair (the kind that would flop over his brown eyes when he really got into his music) and a lean, lanky physique, he had the ladies (and quite a few gents, too) dancing to his syncopated rhythms in music halls across the country. A gifted pianist and band and orchestra leader, he had a string of hits that lasted from 1932 until 1942, including "Let's Fall in Love," before entering the navy as a lieutenant. Seemingly, the man had everything going for him, until he was struck by sudden illness (leukemia). His lavish, high society life came to a quick end. There you have the unforgettable, made-for-movie tale of slick and sophisticated Eddy Duchin. (Note: Duchin's son, Peter, carrying on in the same tradition as his beloved father, became a noted musician too.) (Everett)

this page: (b. Wladziu Valentino Liberace, 5/16/19, West Allis, Wis., d. 2/4/87) The man certainly had his **LiBerace** detractors, but there was no way one could negate the svengalilike charm Liberace had at his fingertips. As resplendent as a rhinestone-covered peacock, "Lee," as he was known to friends and many fans, strutted on stage in the most ornate costumes, often seated at equally overdecorated pianos where his signature candelabra would always rest. Though his specialty for playing "pop" pieces with a classical sounding edge revolted the upper ranks of performing artists and critics, his intentions certainly had their merits: occasionally one would hear a bona fide classical composition! Born to parents who played the french horn and piano, and raised with siblings who shared his musical inclinations, "Mr. Showmanship," as he would also become known, had a distinct audience; his flamboyant personality made women adore him, but men loathed the very sight of him. The fact that men stayed clear of his performances hardly affected his bank account: he was, at his peak, the highest paid musician/pianist in the world. A favorite tune: "I'll Be Seeing You," which he played at the close of every concert. A favorite saying: "Without the show there's no business." (Wallace Seawell/MPTV)

(b. Barry Alan Pincus, 6/17/46, Brooklyn, N.Y.) After graduating from New York City's Julliard School of Music, our long-limbed Lothario made a name for himself as a composer-writer of successful commercial jingles. He then gained greater notoriety as the piano accompanist for Bette Midler, during her notorious stint playing at the gay Continental baths (also in New York). When Midler landed a recording contract, she enlisted Manilow as a coproducer and arranger; subsequently he signed his own record deal. Unfortunately, his debut album was not a success. However, a follow-up single, "Mandy," was. Manilow's schmaltzy style of musicianship, while not the most innovative or original, resulted in an amazing string of Top 40 hits—including the Oscar-nominated "Ready to Take a Chance Again"(from *Seems Like Old Times*, 1977)—and he dominated "middle-of-the-road" playlists for the rest of the decade. Perhaps it was his easygoing presence together with flashy onstage antics, or the fact that he could select ballads and the occasional uptempo tune (like "Copacabana," which he made into a musical) that made him into such a concert hall/arena-filling attraction. Whatever it was, it's proof that you don't have to be classically handsome to have women clamoring to be in your presence. (Everett)

neil sedaka

(b. 3/13/39, Brooklyn, N.Y.) In high school, Sedaka dated Carole King (then known as Carol Klein) and was already a gifted young pianist and songwriter. His talent won him a scholarship to The Julliard School of Music. While still a teen, he wrote his first hit, "Stupid Cupid," which was recorded by Connie Francis (he was also responsible for her classic, "Where the Boys Are"). The following year he signed with RCA, and one of his first solo hits, "Oh, Carol," was written about guess what relationship? Sedaka's catchy melodies were remarkably evocative of the ups and downs of the teen experience: "Breaking Up Is Hard to Do," "Happy Birthday, Sweet Sixteen," "Next Door to Angel," and "Calendar Girl." When Sedaka sang in his trademark soft, velvety voice, he became the perfect guilt-free teen idol; someone you could definitely take home to meet the folks. But not surprisingly, like all teen balladeers of the period, his work, though no less worthy, was largely ignored by record buyers when music tastes changed in the mid-sixties. Then came a stunning career resuscitation in the mid-seventies, beginning with "Laughter in the Rain" (1974), followed by Captain and Tennille's recording of his "Love Will Keep Us Together" (A Grammy winner for 1975's Song of the Year), through to his duet with Elton John on "Bad Blood" (1975) and his remake of "Breaking Up Is Hard to Do." Evidentally, he is still a master of memorable pop songs. (Bettmann/Corbis)

dean martin

this page: (b. Dino Paul Crocetti, 6/7/17, Steubenville, Ohio, d. 12/25/95) Years before he became a member of the rich and famous Hollywood "rat pack," Martin held jobs as a shoe-shine boy, gas station attendant, croupier, and amateur boxer (with the ring name "Kid Crochet"). In 1946, he first worked with comedian Jerry Lewis at the 500 Club in Atlantic City, and their act became a favorite on radio and television, before crossing over into film (beginning with a supporting appearance in *My Friend Irma*, 1948). A wildly successful series of modestly budgeted features followed, many of which contained big hit songs, including Martin's standard "That's Amore!" (*The Caddy*, 1953). Curious side note: fifties audiences, then so unfamiliar with Italian food, mistakenly interpreted the famous introductory line "when the moon hits your eye like a big pizza pie" instead as "big piece of pie." When the pair split in 1956, it was assumed Martin's career would suffer the most, but after a shaky start it became obvious he would survive and indeed, thrive. Movie roles continued unabated and far surpassed earlier efforts in content. Martin also became a nightclub fixture, especially popular in Las Vegas. He was equally at home on weekly television, as the "inebriated" host who welcomed top entertainers and lasciviously cavorted with his famed Golddigger dancers on his self-titled variety series. In fact, Martin was such a popular star that he enjoyed his greatest single success, "Everybody Loves Somebody," the year the Beatles released "A Hard Day's Night." His song actually knocked the group out of the top spot! Damn, these old guys were hard to keep down! (Ken Veeder/MPTV)

opposite: (b. 12/8/25, Harlem, N.Y., d. 5/16/90) He was taught how to tap dance by Bill "Bojangles" Robinson, but, at age three, Davis performed under the name "Silent Sam, the Dancing Midget" (which he got from his father!)—and still went on to become a legendary entertainer! In 1954, his debut album for Decca (*Starring Sammy Davis*) was a surprise number-one hit—quite the accomplishment for a relative newcomer and *especially* for someone who was black. In 1955, he appeared on Broadway for the first time in the show *Mr. Wonderful*—which introduced the hit "Too Close for Comfort"—the same year he lost an eye in an auto accident. Often cited as the first African-American male entertainer popular to both black and white audiences, he also attracted their criticism when he converted to Judaism and for his frequent relationships with white women (including his marriage to Swedish beauty, Mai Britt, in 1960). Davis had only one number-one single, "Candy Man" (1972), written by Leslie Briscusse and Anthony Newley, with whom he also had the hit "What Kind of Fool Am I?" Despite his continued success and consistent high level of entertaining, Davis died nearly penniless. The reasoning: a lifelong weakness for gambling, smoking, and drinking. (Gene Howard/MPTV)

sammy davis jr.

a pair
OF ACEZ

TOM JONES

(b. Thomas Jones Woodward, 6/7/40, Pontyridd, Mid-Glamorgan, Wales) Jones originally performed as Tommy Scott, but his fledgling effort failed to find an audience. But his "new" name, and a follow-up single, "It's Not Unusual," got the attention of English fans—eventually the world's—and didn't let go. A hip-gyrating sensation, Jones's sexy swagger—a more advanced version of Elvis Presley's decade-earlier physical gyrations—was definitely for "adults only." Performing onstage in such a highly sexualized manner, this Welsh wolf's act was far from commonplace. By the seventies—after memorable, sweaty, and loud hits like "What's New Pussycat?," "Delilah," and "Without Love There Is Nothing"—he made a fortune growling and swiveling on the lucrative Las Vegas strip and discontinued active recording. Jones's over-the-top machismo was brought to the attention of a younger, newer audience when his collaboration with the innovative group The Art of Noise—on a remake of Prince's "Kiss"—became a surprise hit in 1988. Since then, the man who for years had female fans throwing keys and underwear at him when he was performing in the sixties and seventies, continues to entertain (but, alas, no more flying undies!) (Gunther/MPTV)

Las Vegaz!

ENGELBERT HUMPERDiNCK

(b. Arnold George Dorsey, 5/2/36, Madras, India) Performing as Gerry Dorsey during the fifties, "The Humpster" (can you believe that nickname?!) first tried a singing career in mainstream pop, but, unfortunately, no one bothered to listen. In the mid-sixties, after battling (and winning) a near fatal bout with tuberculosis, he had exhausted himself and his professional options. His career was rescued by longtime friend Gordon Mills—who had achieved great success working with Tom Jones—and he was relaunched as "Engelbert Humperdinck" (named for the nineteenth-century composer). This time he focused on singing ballads, which quickly resulted in his 1967 hit "Release Me (And Let Me Love Again)." Though Humperdinck's act lacked the "heat" of friendly rival Jones, his fans were just as plentiful and enamored of their mutton chop–sideburned idol. He once joked about his bra-throwing fans, "it's such a waste; none of them ever fit me." He, too, became a formidable presence in Vegas, and over the years has had fun parodying his image—most notably when he sang "Lesbian Seagull" for the soundtrack of *Beavis and Butthead Do America* (1996). (Corbis)

JOHN RAITT

(b. 1/19/17, Santa Ana, Calif.) The father of country/rock music superstar Bonnie Raitt began as a light operatic singer before moving to New York and being given the lead in Rodgers and Hammerstein's classic 1945 musical *Carousel* (after having played Curly in the Chicago-based tour company of R&H's previous groundbreaker *Oklahoma!*). His success in the part made him a major Broadway star, and Raitt appeared in a series of highly regarded though not necessarily blockbuster productions, until he landed the starring role in *Pajama Game*—the Adler-Ross musical also starring Janis Paige—a job that lasted well over two years. In his role he introduced the beautiful "Hey There" and was so well-received he repeated his role in the on-screen version opposite Doris Day—a rare occurrence. Unfortunately, movie musicals were past their peak of popularity, and the brawny balladeer's flirtation with film was short lived; he enjoyed longer term success on television and his beloved stage. (Everett)

KNiGHTZ on BroaDWaY

(b. 12/26/33, Lawrence, Mass.)
After several years working across **ROBERT GOULET**
the border in Canada, playing in a number of touring Broadway shows, Goulet, possibly the hand-somest man to appear on The Great White Way, had an astoundingly successful on-Broadway debut in Lerner and Loewe's *Camelot* (1960). Though playing opposite stellar costars Julie Andrews (Guinevere) and Richard Burton (King Richard), as Sir Lancelot, Goulet had matinee-idol looks—raven black hair, piercing blue eyes, and a formidable physique—and a gorgeous, almost too-masculine-sounding singing voice that made him the toast of the town. With a killer puss like his, would it be long before Hollywood beckoned? No, but unfortunately his initial screen career suffered from a lack of suitable vehicles—though he eventually found work in character parts. Nevertheless, he thrived on television, the stage (notably for his triumphant 1968 Tony—winning role in *The Happy Time*), and as a recording artist (winning the Grammy for Best New Artist in 1962). His two biggest hits are "If Ever I Would Leave You" (from *Camelot*) and "My Love, Forgive Me" (his sole Top 40 single). (Corbis)

nelson eddy

this page: (b. 6/29/01, Providence, R.I., d. 3/6/67) As a young man he learned to sing by listening to opera records, and before entering motion pictures as a singer-actor, Eddy held down jobs ranging from a telephone operator to advertising salesman. Despite not being the most skilled performer, he had a stolid charm and strong baritone voice that, coupled onscreen with the feminine charm and solid soprano voice of Jeanette MacDonald, created the most successful singing partnership on film. *Naughty Marietta* (1935), their first collaboration, introduced one of two oft-parodied duets "Ah, Sweet Mystery of Life" (the second being "Indian Love Call," from *Rose Marie* in 1936). Their string of light opera hits (eight in all) enjoyed favor for only a brief window in time. The onset of World War II changed movie audience's tastes, and their saccharine-edged productions were deemed a touch too sweet. On his own, fair-haired Eddy was responsible for bringing the immortal Cole Porter love song "In the Still of the Night" (from the 1937 film *Rosalie*) to mass audiences. He also brought us his signature song "Shortnin' Bread" (from the 1946 Disney compilation film *Make Mine Music*, where he supplied the voice for the singing Willie the Whale), before appearing in his last film, another light operetta called *Northwest Outpost* (1947). (Photofest)

mario lanza

opposite: (b. Alfred Arnold Cocozza, 1/31/21, Philadelphia, Penn., d. 10/7/59) The brief and legendary career of this sensational and physically dominating entertainer began when, as a high school dropout, the forceful tenor actively sought wealthy patronage in his effort to become, in his own words, "the greatest dramatic opera singer who ever lived." Unfortunately, early attempts were cut short; Lanza was enlisted in the army in 1943. However, he performed for troops, as "The Service Caruso"—named for his idol, Enrico Caruso—and began making a name for himself. In 1948, Lanza made his first and only professional opera stage appearance in *Madame Butterfly* (for two performances). He signed a seven-year film contract with MGM, after being spotted by studio head Louis B. Mayer, but said that the medium made him "nervous." His fears led to a dangerous eating disorder that resulted in major fluctuations in weight. Nevertheless, he was an enormous success and single-handedly reinvigorated the public's interest in opera. His most-remembered song? "Be My Love" from *The Toast of New Orleans* (1950)—where he also looked his best. Most bizarre professional turn? When he recorded the songs for *The Student Prince* (1954) but was fired and replaced by nonsinging actor Edmund Purdom (who lip-synched on the soundtrack). Tired of Hollywood (and stiff tax laws), Lanza retired to Italy in 1957, where he died under mysterious circumstances at only age thirty-eight. Lanza's legacy is unique, though his contribution to recorded music is still debated by critics and historians. (Corbis)

smooth **opera**TORZ

gordon macrae

this page: (b. Albert Gordon MacRae, 3/12/21, East
Orange, N.J., d. 1/24/86) During the forties, fifties, and even into the early sixties, it seemed that any male singer worth his weight in hay played the role of Curly from the musical *Oklahoma!*—but only one man would play in the original film version. That honor went to MacRae, who, before snagging the coveted part, starred opposite Doris Day in five quite likable musicals starting with *Tea for Two* (1950), had a hit NBC radio show, and sang with Harry James at the New York World's Fair in 1939. MacRae also knew how to play the piano, clarinet, and saxophone—*and* was a navigator in the air force. Sadly, by the time MacRae starred in his second Rodgers and Hammerstein screen adaptation, *Carousel* (1956), it would be his last movie musical; the genre was evaporating. Adding to his problems, MacRae was dealing with alcoholism, which resulted in an arrest during filming of the classic picture. After a prolonged battle lasting into the seventies, he was finally able to beat his addiction and sought to counsel other sufferers. From 1941 to 1967, MacRae was married to actress/singer Sheila MacRae (*The Jackie Gleason Show*, 1966–70), with whom he had four children, including the late actress Meredith MacRae (1944–2000) of *Petticoat Junction* fame. (MPTV)

opposite: (b. Harold Clifford Leek, 4/13/17, Gillespie, Ill.) This six-foot-four hunk with a booming baritone voice worked as a singing waiter—and as the "in-house entertainment" for the Douglas Aircraft company (no, not as a singing flight attendant!)—before playing the lead role of Curly in the early London production of *Oklahoma!* Moving to Hollywood in the late forties, he was cast in his first film *The Small Voice* (1948)—a nonsinging part. His big break came when he landed the role of Frank Butler in the hit film version of *Annie Get Your Gun* (1950) opposite Betty Hutton. His manly physique worked well on film, especially when musical roles called for a robust presence. Among his best pictures: *Showboat* (1951), *Kiss Me, Kate* (1953), and *Seven Brides for Seven Brothers* (1954). When studios stopped producing lavish musicals, he gravitated to television, low-budget westerns (no one looked better on horseback!), and action films. Included in his credits is the sci-fi cult classic *The Day of the Triffids* (1963) and his role of Clayton Farlow on the television soap opera *Dallas* (1981–91). The latter reinvigorated interest in his singing career, and he began performing in concert and recording again. (Corbis)

HOWARD KEEL

BEEFY BARiTONEZ

screen Gemz

David SOUL

(b. David Solberg, 8/28/43, Chicago) As the son of a minister, professor of history, and religious affairs advisor, Soul spent his early childhood living between America (South Dakota) and Berlin (where father was active in postwar reconstruction). During his high school years, Soul was back on U.S. soil, and he showed promise as a talented baseball player. Upon graduation, Soul was offered a contract with the Chicago White Sox but turned down the offer to accompany his family on a diplomatic mission to Mexico. It was there that the young man was first turned on by music—and the thought of entertaining. Soul moved to Minneapolis and got work performing because he was, as he put it, "the only blond, blue-eyed Norwegian who could sing Mexican folk songs." (That's a safe bet!) He married his high school sweetheart in 1964 but divorced quickly thereafter. About the same time, his acclaim began as a folksinger, and he was an opening act for The Lovin' Spoonful, The Byrds, and Frank Zappa. For a time during the sixties, he also performed as "The Covered Man," donning a mask for the entire time he was onstage. Appearing frequently on *The Merv Griffin Show*, the act was all the rage, but his popularity plummeted when he finally demasked himself. By the seventies, he turned to acting, beginning with the TV series *Here Come the Brides* (opposite fellow teen idol Bobby Sherman), and the move overtook his singing career. However, the great fame he attracted playing Ken Hutchinson in *Starsky and Hutch* helped to propel his release, "Don't Give Up on Us Baby" straight to the top of the charts in 1979. (Michael Ochs)

TaB HunTeR

(b. Arthur Gelien, 7/11/31, New York City) In 1946, hunky Hunter lied about his age in order to be admitted to the Coast Guard (he was fifteen; you needed to be sixteen). In 1950, this untrained actor—who was a champion ice skater and horse rider—had his film debut in *The Lawless* and by the middle of the decade he was quite successful. Adding *Battle Cry* (1955), a film role that he won over James Dean, and *Burning Hills* (1956), one of two films in which he costarred with Natalie Wood, to his growing list of popular films, this star shot through the roof when he recorded and released "Young Love" in 1957. Though Sonny James and The Crew Cuts made their own covers of the song, Hunter's version was the winner; his stayed six weeks atop the charts and established him as an all-around entertainment force. Perfect casting came when he played Joe Hardy, the singing baseball player in *Damn Yankees* (1958). Combining an easygoing manner and classic good looks, Hunter is also one of the first to poke fun at his enduring status as an iconic all-American male ideal (*Polyester*, 1981). (Corbis)

michael Damian

(b. Michael Damian Weir, 4/26/62, San Diego, Calif.) Beginning in 1981, Damian was cast in the highly rated daytime drama *The Young and the Restless*. His run lasted an astounding eighteen years, when his character, rather cleverly, left in 1998 to "go on tour." From the start, delectable Damian played perfectly to man-starved soap opera audiences, and he won a number of young talent awards for his "efforts." But Damian was more than just a pumped-up plaything; for as long as he was acting, Damian was a working musician. By the time he landed a recurring role as "The Fly Man" (a rock musician-turned-lounge singer) in the primetime comedy *The Facts of Life*, his music career was set to take center stage. With his increased visibility, Damian's 1989 release, "Rock On," became a huge number-one hit. For a moment, he seemed to have it all. But the momentum did not last and, one by one, things fell by the wayside. Today, Damian still acts (he was a hit on stage in *Joseph and the Amazing Technicolor Dreamcoat*, a production you will hear named again!) and records. In a Dorian Gray twist, he looks (to many) even better and certainly more buff now than when we first laid eyes on him. (Michael Benabib/Retna)

JOHN Travolta

(b. 2/18/54, Englewood, N.J.) The youngest of six children, Italian-Irish Travolta dropped out of high school to pursue acting and appeared in a number of advertisements, including a memorable commercial for the armed forces. Things were progressing nicely and manageably until this nonchalant six-foot-two charmer (who was titillatingly nicknamed "Bone" as a youth) got the part of boisterous Vinnie Barbarino in the TV sitcom *Welcome Back, Kotter.* And the rest was, as they say, history. His popularity was so overwhelming that fans of the bad boy with the beaming smile begged for more. So it was inevitable that in 1976 he would also launch a so-called recording career. Though no one could truthfully state that Travolta was even a marginal singer, the minor success of his first release, the smarmy tune "Let Her In," proved that fans were willing to tolerate second-rate product. After Travolta became a movie superstar with *Saturday Night Fever,* which led to his taking the lead in *Grease,* he confounded music purists by scoring two top-five hits off of *Grease*'s soundtrack, including the number-one "You're the One That I Want," written especially for the movie. (Notably, Travolta shared the mike on both tunes with Australian songbird Olivia Newton-John.) Post-*Grease,* of Travolta's many talents (which now count writing among them) singing seems to have faded away. As far as can be determined, no one appears to mind the loss. (Gene Trindl/MPTV)

opposite: (b. 9/25/68, Philadelphia, Penn.) Smith is six-foot-two inches of "fresh" princely charm. As a young man, he got that nickname—"fresh prince"—because of his charismatic demeanor, winning smile, and forthright manner. Smith was also a bit of a clown, and he met his music partner, Jeff Townes, at a party, only after realizing that Townes was the only person laughing at his tirade of middling jokes. The two became fast friends, and since both had an interest and aptitude for hip-hop music, they formed the duo, DJ Jazzy Jeff and the Fresh Prince. With relatively quick dispatch, they released a series of lyrically inoffensive urban cuts—including the first Grammy-winning rap song, "Parents Just Don't Understand," which separated the two from their erstwhile peers. In 1989, smack dab in the middle of his chart run, Smith began work on the television series *Fresh Prince of Bel-Air*, in which the affable young star basically portrayed himself. The show lasted six years, when it was usurped by Smith's movie career. After appearing in some of the most successful films of all time—*Independence Day, Men in Black*—he is, at twenty-million-dollars-plus per film, among the highest paid stars in Hollywood. Smith's music career did not disappear after he hit the cameras; with three number ones—"(Theme from) The Men in Black," "Gettin' Jiggy wit It," and "(Theme from) Wild, Wild West"—his post-picture recording popularity actually surpassed what came before. (John Spellman/Retna)

this page: (b. 6/5/71, Boston, Mass.) This hunk

mark wahlberg

hates being referred to by his former performance name, "Marky Mark." It is a constant reminder to him of what a person will do, in relative youth, to get ahead in the competitive world of show business. (Are you listening, Vanilla Ice and Snow?) After dropping out of high school, Wahlberg became an early member of brother Donnie's boy-band, New Kids on the Block, but left the group because of their too-squeaky-clean image. However, the elder sibling still helped to secure a separate record deal for his "delinquent" brother. Wahlberg's new handlers sensed a pot of gold underneath their bad boy's exterior—and they were so right! Years of minor incursions with the law landed Mark in prison, where this former boney Bostonian passed the time by working out, becoming quite sensationally buff-and-ruff. Wahlberg used his heart-palpitating physique to power over the rest of the competition. Onstage, losing his shirt (did he even own one?) and dropping his pants, he was a musical performance conundrum; though lacking in singing ability and with only a modicum of dancing ability, he and his "funky bunch" had two big hits, including the chart-topper "Love Sensation," which owed a great deal of its success to the stellar vocals of Loleatta Holloway. However, becoming an underwear model extraordinaire—which, literally, turned that market "inside-out"—only inflamed critics who felt that Wahlberg was more interested in image than content. Wahlberg proved to be a much better actor than singer and combined the two with middling success in *Rock Star* (2001). However, as is evident in many of his movie roles (especially 1998's *Boogie Nights*), Wahlberg still seems to have a problem keeping his clothes on. But I don't hear any complaints! (Steve Granitz/Retna)

this page: (b. Desiderio Alberto Arnaz Y De Acha III, 3/2/17, Santiago, Cuba, d. 12/2/86) His father was mayor of Santiago, Cuba, but during the 1934 Batista revolt was unseated from his office. The family, after the loss of their power and wealth, sought refuge in Miami. In 1936, Arnaz was hired to play for "The King of Latin Music" Xavier Cugat, but by the following year the heartthrob left to form his own band. His immediate success (he is considered responsible for starting a worldwide Latin "craze" well over sixty years before Ricky Martin reintroduced the same) led Broadway producers to cast him in the show *Too Many Girls,* which was followed by a move to Hollywood so that Arnaz could film the motion picture version. There he met comedienne Lucille Ball. They fell in love, had a whirlwind courtship, and married in 1940. Ten years later, they formed Desilu and began producing the show *I Love Lucy,* which began as the radio show *My Favorite Husband* based on a book entitled *Mr. and Mrs. Cugat* (yes, *that* Mr. Cugat!). Their dashing son Desi Jr. (or rather, Desiderio Alberto Arnaz IV)—whose "birth" was a celebrated national television event—also had a run at music teen-idol status back in the late sixties when he formed the singing trio Dino (the handsome offspring of Dean Martin), Desi, & Billy, and courted pretty actresses Victoria Principal and Patty Duke. (Underwood & Underwood/Corbis)

opposite: (b. Enrique Jose Martin Morales, 12/24/71, San Juan, P.R.) Martin started acting and singing in grade school. By age ten, he had auditioned for the infamous Latin boy-band Menudo (which unceremoniously would drop its members as soon as they turned age sixteen), but did not make the grade until turning twelve. For five years, from 1984 to 1989, he and his agile amigos romped across the globe, breaking the hearts of little girls from one country to the next. It was obvious from the start that little Ricky loved the spotlight and we loved seeing him in it; as he grew into a young man that spotlight grew ever larger. After vacating his place in Menudo's everchanging lineup, Martin started his solo recording career. Intermittently he was seen acting: in the Mexican soap opera *Alcanzar una Estrella* and portraying a singing bartender on the top American sudser *General Hospital.* All was going well, but success was generally limited to the Spanish-speaking markets. For Martin this was not enough. In true tropical "heatwave" fashion, Martin carefully planned his assault on domestic shores. First he sent temperatures soaring with his scorching appearance on the 1999 Grammy Award telecast. Even such nonplussed megatalents as Madonna remarked that they had not seen, heard, or felt such a sizzling performance in ages. His moment in the sun set off a worldwide frenzy of media attention, culminating in the release of his smash self-titled English-language record debut. At the center of the maelstrom, the single "Living la Vida Loca" became Columbia Record's biggest-selling single. Even the clothes he wore became hot fashion news; no one was a better calling card for stretch T-shirts and tight pants! But with all flare-ups there are the expected cool-downs. Dogged by rumors of his sexuality, the release of lackluster follow-up product, not to mention a crushing onslaught of equally easy-on-the-eye south of the border talent (Enrique Iglesias, Marc Anthony, Carlos Ponce, et al.), Martin has seen his sizzle simmer down. Nevertheless, we have not seen the last of him. Thank God for that! (Reuters/Corbis)

inTerNatioNaL maLe

JULIO IGLESIAS

(b. 9/23/43, Madrid, Spain) Many consider him the "father" of Latin music hunks, and he is certainly the sire of one of his own—gorgeous Enrique. But did you know that with over two hundred million records sold, Iglesias stands as one of the most successful recording artists of all time? Surprisingly, he trained as a lawyer first and was a professional soccer player before severe injuries from a 1963 car accident put an end to his sports career. While he was recuperating from his injuries, he learned to play the guitar and began writing songs. He entered a music contest and won first prize, and that led to a contract with a Spanish record label. For the entirety of the seventies, he worked only in Europe, becoming a massive success by singing in a number of languages including French, Italian, Spanish, and English. In 1981, he had his first big United Kingdom hit, "Begin the Beguine" (a remake of the Artie Shaw big band classic), and followed it with a deliberate attempt to enter the lucrative American market. The year 1984 saw hit-making collaborative efforts with country great Willie Nelson ("To All the Girls I've Loved Before") and pop icon Diana Ross ("All of You"). His enormous and lengthy tenure at the top of his field—which continues on a lesser degree today—is evidence that domestic acts do not hold an absolute monopoly on record turntables. (Doc Pele/Retna)

enrique iGLesias

(b. 5/8/75, Madrid, Spain) How do you succeed in the recording business without *necessarily* trying? 1) Your father, Julio, is an amazingly successul recording artist; 2) You also possess a great singing voice; 3) You secretly had aspirations to be a singer ever since you were a teen; and possibly the most significant 4) You happen to be one of the most attractive and sexy men on the planet. (Iglesias's kisser has graced over two hundred magazines!) Young Iglesias did, by the way, have to earn his stripes. His parents divorced when he was seven—right about the time when *padre* was launching his assault on the western world. Early on there was talk of a rivalry between parent and child, fueled by the dashing son's comment, "When I have children, I'll leave work to one side for a while, something my father never did." To Enrique's credit, his rise to fame in the American market was much quicker than that of his father; no doubt this was precipitated by the late-nineties influx of other Latin music acts, most notably his rival Ricky Martin. (Scott Teitler/Retna)

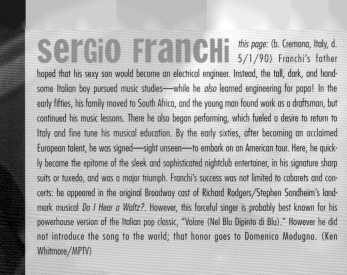

serGio FrancHi

this page: (b. Cremona, Italy, d. 5/1/90) Franchi's father hoped that his sexy son would become an electrical engineer. Instead, the tall, dark, and handsome Italian boy pursued music studies—while he *also* learned engineering for papa! In the early fifties, his family moved to South Africa, and the young man found work as a draftsman, but continued his music lessons. There he also began performing, which fueled a desire to return to Italy and fine tune his musical education. By the early sixties, after becoming an acclaimed European talent, he was signed—sight unseen—to embark on an American tour. Here, he quickly became the epitome of the sleek and sophisticated nightclub entertainer, in his signature sharp suits or tuxedo, and was a major triumph. Franchi's success was not limited to cabarets and concerts: he appeared in the original Broadway cast of Richard Rodgers/Stephen Sondheim's landmark musical *Do I Hear a Waltz?*. However, this forceful singer is probably best known for his powerhouse version of the Italian pop classic, "Volare (Nel Blu Dipinto di Blu)." However he did not introduce the song to the world; that honor goes to Domenico Modugno. (Ken Whitmore/MPTV)

opposite: (b. 9/14/59, Konigsberg, Norway) Many will probably not recognize this cutie by name (yet, upon hearing it, who could forget it?), but most certainly would have seen his face as part of the mid-eighties pop group, A-Ha. The trio (which formed in 1982) did not do well with the initial release of the hit single "Take on Me." However, rerecording the track and the simultaneous launch of a revolutionary accompanying video sent the tune on its trajectory to the top. Though all three members of the group were sublime Scandinavian lads, Harket stood out with his chiseled jawline and alluring Norwegian accent. (It also helped that he portrayed the pencil-drawn hero in the video.) The band joined the ranks of other teen idol groups of the era—Duran Duran and Spandau Ballet among them—but success was fleeting and they disbanded late in the decade. Today, Harket is still a great-looking "older" man and continues to record as a solo act. He has also made limited attempts at a Norwegian movie career. (Tim Bauer/Retna)

morten Harket

maurice chevalier

this page: (b. 9/12/1888, Paris, France, d. 1/1/72) By birth, Chevalier is the oldest entertainer in this book, and, by starting at the turn of the century, is the one who began his career earliest. He was one of ten children and was a circus acrobat who had an injury that forced a rethinking of options. He turned to singing and light comedy and became quite popular and worked at the Folies Bèrgere. During World War I he was drafted into the army and captured by the Germans. Ever resourceful, he learned to speak English while in prison camp. After liberation, he returned to the stage more sophisticated than ever in his now-familiar boater hat and performing sing-song style. Hollywood called, and in Chevalier's first film *Love Parade* (1929) he introduced a signature tune, "Louise." Arriving at the same time as talkies, he had an accent (and oh-so-pouty lips!) that helped him to become one of the world's biggest stars. While living in Paris at the onset of World War II, he performed only twice—at the behest of German occupation forces (resulting in unfounded rumors of Nazi sympathizing). Following the war, he reemerged even *more* sophisticated. He made an indelible mark as a character actor in a number of prestigious pictures, including *Gigi* (Oscar, Best Picture, 1958). In it he sang his last great recording, "Thank Heaven for Little Girls" and, at age seventy, was given a special Academy Award for his "contribution to entertainment." Chevalier was, incidentally, a twice Oscar-nominated actor. This dapper Gaul gained quite the reputation as a "rake" over his lifetime, prompting early costar Jeanette MacDonald to once quip, "He was the fastest derriere pincher in Hollywood!" (Everett)

opposite: (b. Ivo Livo, 10/13/21, Monsummano Alto, Italy, d. 11/9/91) Montand was one of the last men to work on-screen with Marilyn Monroe (off-screen they were also purported to have had an affair). The film was George Cukor's *Let's Make Love* (1960), and it introduced the sexy singing star to audiences at that point only familiar with him as the attractive husband of Oscar-winning actress Simone Signoret. They were together until her death in 1985. Montand's family emigrated to France to escape Mussolini's rule when he was a teen; as a dashing young man, he took work singing in Parisian night spots. It was while performing in one of those boîtes that he was discovered by Edith Piaf. Though acclaimed as a singer, Montand—who took his name from his mother's call "Ivo monta!" (translating roughly into "Come upstairs, Ivo!")—gained greater notoriety as a cynically mannered actor and political activist. Three films worth a look (and listen): *Jean de Florette* (1986), Costa-Gavra's *Z* (1969), and the musical *On a Clear Day You Can See Forever* (1970) with Barbra Streisand. (Everett)

yves montand

Jan & Dean

this page, left to right: Dean Torrence (b. 3/10/40, Los Angeles, Calif.) and Jan Berry (b. 4/3/41, Los Angeles, Calif.) This pretty pair of penultimate California surfer dudes met while playing on their high school football team—Berry was a tight end; Torrence, a wide receiver. As was often the "custom" back then, teammates sang in the showers after a game. (Isn't that sweet?!) The pair discovered, along with a third student, Arnie Ginsburg, that their voices were quite compatible and formed a trio. They had a minor hit, "Jennie Lee," almost immediately, but Dean was drafted before the single's release. Hence it is credited to the duo, Jan and Arnie. This union proved short lived, and upon Torrence's return, he and Berry reunited. For four years, the tanned twosome enjoyed marginal success. Then, in 1963, they released their (only) number-one hit, "Surf City," and the sound, so evocative of sunny and sandy California (thanks to the writing talents of Brian Wilson of The Beach Boys), propelled them into the front ranks of pop stardom and, of course, teen idol worship. They were well known for their songs about cars and drag racing—including "Dead Man's Curve" (1964). Thus it is ironic that a paralyzing auto accident, involving twenty-five-year-old Berry in 1966, would effectively end their partnership. Torrence went on to work as a graphic designer, credited with developing the logo for the group Chicago and winning a Grammy for Best Album Cover of 1971 for *Pollution*. After a partial recovery, Berry rejoined forces with Torrence in 1978, and with the newly regrouped Beach Boys, went on a totally bitchin' tour! (Everett)

everly Brothers

opposite, left to right: Don Everly (b. 2/1/37, Brownie, Ky.) and Phil Everly (b. 1/19/39, Chicago, Ill.) As the musically inclined children of country singers Ike and Margaret, the Everly boys appeared on their parents' radio show throughout the forties and fifties. As they matured in the latter decade, strains of rock 'n roll were incorporated with the music of their bucolic roots. One early standout, the single "Bye, Bye Love," was a hit because it had a more sanitized sound than the music of fellow rock artists like Elvis Presley—and was therefore more acceptable to parents. In 1960, their first release for Warner Bros., the sophisticated and introspective "Cathy's Clown," was a musical about-face for the act and *all* recorded music (previous pop cuts tended to be rather light in lyrical content). It became an instant classic. The following year, both brothers served short stints in the marines. Unfortunately, upon their return, Don developed a serious drug habit—owing to the strain of performing—and tensions grew severe between the siblings. They officially broke up in 1973 and would meet only once in the years that followed (for their father's funeral) before reuniting in 1983. They continue appearing together to this day. (Everett)

DYnamic DUOZ

GO WEST

Richard Drummie and Peter Cox (b. 11/17/55, London, England) This attractive toothy twosome, who met in 1974, worked as songwriters (with Peter Frampton, and others) before forming Go West in 1982. They released their first album in 1985 and were an instant success in native England, but it would take a few years before they could say the same for themselves in the United States. That triumph came when the single "King of Wishful Thinking" became a surprise hit off of the soundtrack from the smash movie *Pretty Woman* (1990). What was also *not* a guarantee from the start? The same pinup boy status they enjoyed in the United Kingdom. Despite their good looks—Cox, the dashing, dark blond lead vocalist, and Drummie, the adorable, wavy-brown-haired instrumentalist—both were well into their thirties (egads!) when they began to scale domestic charts. Mind you, they did have a number of fans who were as fond of their physical traits as for their music, which was always well crafted and produced. Though they were still very close friends, after a final tour, the two separated in 1993. (Waring Abbott/Michael Ochs)

from left to right: Daryl Hall (b. Daryl Franklin Hohl, 10/11/48, Pottstown, Pa.) and John Oates (b. 4/7/49, New York City) Both were Temple University students when they met in the late sixties. Physically and spiritually, blue-eyed Hall and mustachioed Oates were the perfect musical bookends. They were discovered by legendary entertainment mogul Tommy Mottola (who, at the time, was working for Chappell Music), and he became their manager and set about marketing the duo's unique blend of R&B/pop music. They scored with a series of "soulful" mid-seventies hits—"Sara, Smile," "She's Gone," and "Rich Girl"—but by the start of the following decade had an even greater impact on the charts with skillfully crafted uptempo pop—"Kiss on My List," "I Can't Go for That (No Can Do)," and "Maneater." Gone also was the neo-glam rock look that they favored in the early years (complete with blush, eyeshadow, and skimpy, torn T-shirts), and in its place was an unadulterated pair, now fancying skinny ties and pointy shoes, performing at the peak of their talents. They were so successful during this period that the twosome became the most popular recording duo of all time, surpassing previous title holders The Everly Brothers. (Michael Ochs)

Hall & Oates

this page, left to right: Daniel Jones (b. 7/22/73, London, England) and Darren Hayes (b. 5/8/72, Brisbane, Australia) Sexy, dark-haired vocalist Hayes (who is a natural blond) met sweet and shy multi-instrumentalist Jones (who stayed a blond) when the former auditioned as lead singer for the latter's then-current band, Red Edge, in 1993. Hayes got the job. However, the two quickly tired of performing unoriginal work and decided to separate from the group and form their own duo. Taking inspiration for their name from celebrated author Anne Rice's vampire books, Savage Garden became Australian superstars in 1996, when their single "I Want You" became the biggest single of the year. The following year, that success was repeated worldwide. (In fact, the song was so popular in America it was picked up by soft drink maker Coca-Cola to promote their cherry cola.) This was topped by subsequent self-penned single releases, "Truly, Madly, Deeply" and "I Knew I Loved You." Sly Hayes (who loves wearing tight see-through shirts) and boyish Jones (who, surprisingly, prefers to sleep in the nude) separated in late 2001. Say it isn't so! (Robin Sellick/Headpress/Retna)

opposite, left to right: Evan Mitchell and Jaron David Lowenstein (both born 3/8/74, Atlanta, Ga.) It's likely an act like this comes along once in a lifetime. They are identical twins who can write, play, and sing songs, *and* who both look like handsome leading men (think of Jared Leto mixed with a young George Clooney or Rob Lowe). But don't call them pop artists; they specialize in an updated folk/rock sound. Whatever category they fall into, the two are sure to attract attention. They began performing music together while in their teens. But there was every possibility that the hunky pair—who were high school captains of their basketball, tennis, and soccer teams as well as semipro baseball players—would have stayed away from the music business altogether if Evan (the five-minute-older brother) had not become a fan of musician Elvis Costello. (Evan positively doted on Costello's work.) They gained local notoriety in Atlanta, after disc jockeys informed the brothers that they would play a song only from "a major label" and released their first album of tunes on their own A Major Label. (Very cute, boys!) Frustrated with covering other artists' works, this pair of siblings turned to penning their own compositions including their first top-twenty hit "Crazy for the Girl" (which gained popularity on TV's *Dawson's Creek*). The two are strict observers of the Jewish faith and never perform after sundown on Friday. Such good boys! (Borucki/Retna)

LeiF GarreTT

opposite: (b. 11/8/61, Hollywood, Calif.) With a father working as a Hollywood cameraman, mother a scriptwriter, and sister a TV actress (she played Dodie in *My Three Sons*), doe-eyed Garrett was destined to also find a place in showbiz. Beginning at age five, he appeared in the cult film fave *Walking Tall* (1973), both sequels, and dozens of other projects, before concentrating his skills on music. Initially, his recording career was little more than remakes of early sixties pop songs—including "Surfin' USA" and "Runaround Sue"—but his biggest hit was an original disco song "I Was Made for Dancing" (1978). Maybe his hair was a little too long and his pants a little too tight—especially for those not accustomed to boys being so obvious about their sex appeal—but this Scotti Brothers—produced-and-packaged teenybopper heartthrob had prepubescent girls eating out of his hands and could do no wrong. (We also have him to thank for making skateboarding a craze.) Tragically, a few short years after his peak, he was responsible for an auto accident that left a friend paralyzed. The gentleman won a lawsuit against the singer for a whopping $7.1 million dollars, resulting in Garrett's bankruptcy. A personal quote: "Never believe your own press." Amen to that. (Michael Ochs)

this page, from left to right: (Clarke) Isaac (guitar) (b. 11/17/80), Zac(hary Walker) (drums) (b. 10/22/85), and **Hanson** (Jordan) Taylor (keyboard) (b. 3/14/83) all born Tulsa, Okla. This trio of ragamuffins took the music world by storm in 1997, with their skillfully crafted pop ditty and worldwide sensation "MMMBop" (which reached number-one in twenty-seven countries!). Growing up the siblings were inspired, musically, by listening to Time-Life compilations of classic fifties and sixties recordings, though their compositions are far more reminiscent of the sixties-seventies "bubble gum" sound of The Osmonds, Bobby Sherman, and The Jackson Five. Performing together since 1992—when Zac was only six!—they were deemed a hard sell, and it took a number of years to find a suitable label. With all of them just *barely* in their teens, Mercury signed them and set about to market their young charges with the album, *Middle of Nowhere*. Their nonthreatening, nonsexual presence was quickly embraced by equally pure young female fans—who threw themselves at the threesome in droves. But youthful fame can be fleeting; after three years passed between their first and second album, *This Time Around*, they lost a huge number of followers in the interim. Although the album was well received and reviewed, this time around there were no takers. (Youri Lenquette/Retna)

59

michael BOLTON

(b. Michael Bolotin, 2/26/53, New Haven, Conn.) This singer began recording under his real name in 1975, and was immediately compared, vocally, to the great Joe Cocker. Bolton recorded with a band during the seventies, and by the eighties he turned to composing and cowrote the Laura Branigan hit "How Am I Suppose to Live without You?" (which he later rerecorded himself). When he decided to go solo, he didn't have much luck until he changed from singing rock songs to soulful ballads—which made far better use of his husky, yearning voice. By the late eighties, long locks and all, this blue-eyed beefcake dominated pop and adult contemporary charts. The first number-one hit for this neck-straining, vein-popping vocalist was his own remake of "Without You," and his biggest single to date was 1993's "Said I Love You But I Lied," which stayed atop the adult contemporary listing a whopping twelve weeks. Although he hasn't charted with the same regularity in the last few years, he remains a highly popular entertainer. But he ran into one major glitch. When the courts decided that one of Bolton's hits, "Love Is a Wonderful Thing," plagiarized an earlier Isley Brothers tune, he was ordered to pay $5 million in damages. Ouch! However, the most important verdict is still pending: Is buff Bolton handsomer as he appears now, shorn of his Samson tresses, or in days of old when his hair made women weak and men cringe? (Ed Geller/Globe)

BiLLY raY CYRUS

(b. 8/25/61, Flatwoods, Ky.) He stomped his way into fan's hearts, but Cyrus is *so* hunky it's hard to take him seriously as a singer. He seems more like an untrained Chippendale dancer! As a youngster, Cyrus sang with his father's gospel quartet and his mother's bluegrass group before even entering school. As a teen, he started a band called Sly Dog (named after his one-eye pet bulldog) and sang regularly at an Ironton, Ohio, bar that burnt to the ground, taking with it all the group's music equipment. Viewing it as a sign to leave the music biz, Cyrus moved to Los Angeles and became a car salesman. Two years later, fed up with a job that was going nowhere, he returned to Kentucky, reformed his group, and made weekly trips to Nashville in search of his big break. It came in 1990, when, as country great Reba McIntire's opening act, he was discovered by talent scouts in Louisville, Kentucky. He got a record deal with Mercury, and his 1992 single "Achy Breaky" became a big, big hit and dance sensation (and was named the Country Music Association's Single of the Year). Perhaps most important, the mullet haircut suddenly became (marginally) acceptable. Today, with a full beard and moustache to go along with the infamous cut, Cyrus has added acting to his resume, appearing as the lead in a syndicated series called *Doc*. (Steve Granitz/Retna)

Kris Kristofferson (b. 6/22/36, Brownsville, Tex.)

The son of an air force general, Kristofferson (who was a helicopter pilot in Vietnam) has led a complicated life. A renowned composer responsible for the classics, "Help Me Make It through the Night" (Grammy winner for Best Country Song of 1971) and Janis Joplin's landmark recording, "Me and Bobby McGee"—he was a Rhodes scholar, was offered a position as an English literature professor, but dropped out of academia to concentrate on music. Taking a gamble, he moved to Nashville in 1965 and worked as a janitor to make ends meet. Things clicked by the late sixties, and the dreamy, blue-eyed stud with a devil-may-care attitude soon became one of the hottest properties in showbiz. The sexy, now-bearded singer also began his film career in 1971 and married country music artist Rita Coolidge in 1973. Barbra Streisand chose him to star opposite her in the 1976 remake of *A Star Is Born*. In many ways the role of the self-destructive singer had many similarities to the real life Kristofferson: he too had a serious alcohol addiction that nearly ruined his professional and private life (effectively leading to his divorce from Coolidge in 1980). The same year of his split with the popular singer his acting career was thrown off course by his starring role in *Heaven's Gate*, deemed at the time to be the most expensive flop in movie history. But all that is many years past, and Kristofferson has beaten his bad habits and continues to sing, compose, and act. (Michael Putland/Retna)

MICHAEL MCDONALD

(b. 12/2/52, St. Louis, Mo.) Here is another sexy, bearded, and blue-eyed singer who helped to bridge the gap between rock and soul music. As a member of The Doobie Brothers—from 1977 to their farewell concert in 1982—McDonald took the group's earlier boogie sound, merged it with his distinctive plaintive baritone voice, and ushered in the band's most successful period, with hit songs like "What a Fool Believes" (a 1979 Grammy winner that McDonald also wrote) and "Takin' It to the Streets." Before joining up with the band, he also sang backup with another innovative group, Steely Dan; *after* leaving The Doobies, he enjoyed a solo chart hit with "I Keep Forgettin' (Every Time You Are Near)" and his Patti LaBelle duet "On My Own" (which, notably, went to number-one on both the pop and soul charts). McDonald also contributed to work by other artists, ranging from Donna Summer and Christopher Cross to Aretha Franklin and Kenny Loggins. No doubt he would have enjoyed more fruits for his labors had he not been such a perfectionist. He labored over three years between solo releases, cancelling another, and his career may have suffered as a result. (Gary Gershoff/Retna)

singing

COWBOYZ

eddy arnold

opposite: (b. Richard Edward Arnold, 5/15/18, Henderson, Tenn.) Because so much of this man's work charted long before many of us were even born, Arnold's contribution to the recording industry has largely been forgotten (except by music historians). However, well in advance of the likes of Garth Brooks and Elvis Presley (who inherited Arnold's manager, the legendary Colonel Tom Parker), the "Tennessee Plowboy" (a nickname that had *everything* to do with his early years working as an extremely poor farmhand) was on his way to becoming one of the most successful acts in country music and a founding father of its modern sound—and what a "daddy" he was! At well over six feet, broad as a doorway, and handsome as a movie star, Arnold had a career that spanned seven decades(!), amassing 145 chart hits. These hits, both country and pop, include at least one truly memorable classic: "Make the World Go Away" (which, by combining lush urban orchestrations and a down-home flavor, was cleverly termed the very first "countrypolitan" hit). His record sales were in excess of eighty-five million records, and he became the first country artist to be given his own television variety show (*Eddy Arnold Time* 1952–56). Arnold learned how to play guitar from his mother (his father died when he was eleven) and continues to perform today—a notable exception that music superstardom can last a lifetime. (Michael Ochs)

GARTH BROOKS

this page: (b. Troyal Garth Brooks, 2/7/62, Tulsa, Okla.) As a young athlete Brooks received a scholarship to Oklahoma State University. While in college, he sang at night and was a popular attraction. After graduation he embarked on a full-time music career instead of using his advertising degree. In 1988, Brooks signed with Capitol Records, the same label his mother, the late country artist Colleen Carroll, had recorded for in the fifties. His first album, simply titled *Garth Brooks*, was well received and sold well, but his second release, *No Fences*, became the first major benchmark of his career. Eventually selling in excess of sixteen million copies, it became the biggest-selling country album of all time. From thereon his career became one long list of superlatives: *Ropin' the Wind*, his third album, became the first to debut simultaneously at number-one on both the pop and country charts—a feat he has repeated on successive releases. In 1996, with sales of over two million tickets, his country tour became the most successful of all time. In addition to winning dozens of top honors, he was named the Artist of the Decade by both the AMA (American Music Awards) and CMA (Country Music Association). With cumulative total sales surpassing one hundred million, he is the biggest-selling solo artist since Elvis Presley. The reason for his popularity is shockingly simple: his work is heartfelt, introspective, at times outspoken, and his manner, soft-spoken. In order to spend more time with his family and pursue other interests, the teddy bear titan of country music has announced his "retirement" on a number of occasions but, rather quizically, continues to perform and remains a giant presence in entertainment. (Lynn McAfee/Retna)

this page: (b. 5/18/52, Poteet, Tex.) Talented, dignified, *and* drop-dead gorgeous, Strait revolutionized country music well before Garth Brooks was given the credit (in fact, Brooks cites Strait as his inspiration). It all began when the handsome ranch worker (his family owned two thousand acres of land) enlisted for a three-year stint in the army and was sent to Hawaii. While listening to country music radio amidst the tropical splendor, he taught himself to play the guitar, joined up with a group of fellow servicemen, and performed for troops. Returning to the mainland, he set about finding work in his now-familiar outfit of cowboy boots, pressed Wrangler jeans, starched western shirt, and the all-important white cowboy hat. Initially he was perceived as too country looking, but he became *the* forerunner of country music's hot "hat acts"—which includes every male performer from Brooks to Clint Black and Tim McGraw. All his releases since 1981 have gone gold or higher, including his biggest seller, the soundtrack for *Pure Country*, in which he put his leading man looks to proper use. (Beth Gwinn/Retna)

opposite: (b. Samuel Timothy McGraw, 5/1/67, Delhi, La.) If you still have an **TiM McGraw** impression that male country artists are no more than barefoot, banjo-strumming yokels, you're obviously not looking at the right men. I mean, could this guy get any sexier—his arms any bigger? his chest any broader? or his waist any smaller?! Brought up by his mother and stepfather (his real father is said to be baseball player Tug McGraw), young Timmy tuned his radio to country music while he worked a tractor (where have you heard that one before?). He carried his love of music with him to college, where, as an athlete and frat boy, he enjoyed partying and "floating kegs" to studying (stop the presses!). Ambivalent about his academic future, he left school to follow in the footsteps of the new breed of buff male country artists, like George Strait, and others. Though he did not have a major country hit until 1994, with *Not a Moment Too Soon*, it was obvious that his looks were instantly popular—and would eventually help expand his audience way beyond its country roots. In 1996, he joined fellow country recording artist Faith Hill on the aptly titled, Spontaneous Combustion Tour. The heat generated by this dashing duo led to their marriage, two daughters, a Grammy award, and oodles of flustered fans of both sexes. (Beth Gwinn/Retna)

COUNTRY BOYZ

JOHN DENVER

(b. Henry John Deutschendorf Jr., 12/31/43, Roswell, N.Mex., d. 10/12/97) Never underestimate the power of simple sentiment and straight-from-the-heart music—it made this man a sought-after composer and solo superstar in the seventies. During the age of Aquarius, Denver sang with the amusingly named group Back Porch Majority (a satellite act of the New Christy Minstrels) and wrote the poignant classic "Leavin' on a Jet Plane" (which was recorded by Peter, Paul, and Mary). In 1969, he began recording on his own and a few years later released the composition that would establish him as the preeminent pop/middle-of-the-road/country artist of his day, "Take Me Home, Country Roads" (1971). The attention Denver received for this effort was repeated and surpassed by his follow-ups, "Sunshine on My Shoulders," "Annie's Song" (written for his wife from 1967–83), "Thank God I'm a Country Boy," and "I'm Sorry." Not surprisingly, since his work was viewed as quite American, he had less luck overseas. Also, critics often lambasted what they felt was banal work. In spite of their indifference, he was amazingly popular among young and old listeners. (Even so, he taught himself to juggle, just in case things didn't work out.) If his music success seemed unexplainable, leading-man status must have appeared even more implausible. Nevertheless, he scored a major movie hit with his first outing *Oh, God* (1980) with George Burns. An avid environmentalist—he was on the board of directors for The Cousteau Society and wrote for its founder the song "Calypso"—he died when his small private plane crashed off a favorite stretch of California coast. (Corbis)

KENNY ROGERS

(b. 8/21/38, Houston, Tex.) Rogers grew up one of seven children in a Houston housing project and would become one of music's most successful performers. He was given the 1990 Horatio Alger Award (you know, the "from rags to riches" guy!) and top honors from HUD, in 1995, for distinguishing himself despite humble beginnings. He first sang with The New Christy Minstrels, then left to form First Edition, a group that had the hits "Just Dropped In (To See What Condition My Condition Was In)" and "Ruby, Don't Bring Your Love to Town," before going solo in the mid-seventies. With his likeable, humble-pie demeanor, and bear-like physique, Rogers was a new kind of music sex symbol (who said they all have to look like Mark McGrath or Donny Osmond?!). As the decade changed over into the eighties, his country-to-pop triumphs escalated, beginning with "Lady," a six-week chart topper. Starting with his hit "The Gambler" (1978), this four-time Grammy winner added acting to his list of activities. Based on the song, he appeared as the lead in a highly rated telefilm; it scored so well in the ratings it spawned four sequels. Rogers was also a onetime pineapple farmer, supplying juicy fruits to Dole, and, with Kenny Rogers Roasters, a profitable restaurateur—until the chain went belly up. (Michael Ochs)

GLEN CAMPBELL

this page: (b. 4/22/36, Delight, Ark.) A brilliant guitarist, standout vocalist, country-and-western music idol, television star (*The Glen Campbell Goodtime Hour*), movie personality (*True Grit*, 1969), and temporary Beach Boy—this down-home dude did it all. The seventh of eight boys and four sisters—all of whom sang and played the guitar—gentle Glen left home at age fourteen to join his uncle Dick's swing band in Albuquerque. At age twenty-four, he moved to Los Angeles and through his talented guitar playing became a much-requested session artist—playing on hits for Frank Sinatra ("Strangers in the Night"), Nat King Cole, Elvis Presley, Ray Charles, and actress Shelly Fabares ("Johnny Angel"). In between time, he toured in place of mentally fatigued Beach Boy Brian Wilson for one year (1965). Then he went out on his own and immediately struck gold with his now-signature song, "Gentle on My Mind" (a 1967 double Grammy winner). His follow-up trio, "By the Time I Get to Phoenix" (also a 1967 double Grammy-winning song), "Wichita Lineman," and "Galveston"—all penned by Jimmy Webb—were pure, unadulterated, and melancholy American music at its best. The album that contained the four cuts, *By the Time I Get to Phoenix*, was named Grammy's Album of the Year in 1968. Though his career slowed in the mid-seventies, he rebounded with two back-to-back smashes "Rhinestone Cowboy" and "Southern Nights"; they were also his first number-one singles. Today, like so many others, he performs regularly in Branson, Missouri—a repository for acts of the past to reconnect with old fans and make favorable impressions on their offspring. (Gunther/MPTV)

opposite: (b. 1/21/42, Lubbock, Tex.) Moving to Atlanta in the mid-fifties, this curly-haired stud taught himself to play the guitar and began writing his own songs. Davis was quoted as saying upon entering college that he "majored in beer and rock and roll." (Men are all alike!) No surprise then that he married at age twenty, had a son, Scotty—whom many songs were written about, including the hit he wrote for Bobby Goldsboro, "Watching Scotty Grow"—and, passing on his studies went totally into music. Other Davis-penned works were recorded by Lou Rawls and Elvis Presley (notably his hit "In the Ghetto"). The pseudo-sexist lyrics to Davis's first major solo hit, "Baby, Don't Get Hooked on Me" (1972), garnered negative attention from feminists, although Davis says any chauvinism was unintentional. An even bigger bad publicity volley was lobbed his way when *Rolling Stone* magazine—in response to his relatively benign pop-country sound—stated that he had "done more to set back the cause of popular music in the seventies than any other figure." Whoa! Davis also dabbled in movies (*North Dallas Forty*, 1979) like his good friend Glen Campbell. The two pals even married the same woman, Sarah Barg: Davis from 1971–76, Campbell from 1976–80. (Everett)

mac Davis

Gene Pitney

this page: (b. 2/17/41, Hartford, Conn.) Pitney had impassioned, wailing vocals so unique that songwriters jumped at the chance to record with him: Burt Bacharach and Hal David had him record early hits "Only Love Can Break a Heart" and "(The Man Who Shot) Liberty Valance" just prior to their working with mainstay Dionne Warwick. When the song "Town without Pity" (from the 1961 film of the same name) was Oscar nominated, Pitney, who recorded the hit, became the first pop artist invited to perform at the esteemed telecast. A gifted composer, guitarist, pianist, and drummer as well, he wrote many compositions for other artists, including massive hits for Ricky Nelson ("Hello, Mary Lou"), The Crystals ("He's a Rebel")—which, coincidentally, kept "Valance" out of the number-one spot—and Bobby Vee ("Rubber Ball"). Like many of the performers of the period, his work was tinged with a country sound, making it somewhat difficult to comfortably categorize. Nevertheless, when the "beatwave" hit in the mid-sixties, Pitney survived the onslaught by collaborating with one of the enemy—The Rolling Stones—and became increasingly popular overseas because of it. (Michael Ochs)

opposite: (b. 9/18/33, Camas, Wash.) This was another singer from the same era known for an impressive voice. Rodgers's creamy, almost effortless vocals made classic hit recordings of "Honeycomb" (his 1957 number-one debut) and "Kisses Sweeter than Wine." He was considered a "rock-'n-roller," but like Pitney and others, his work owed a great deal to the influences of country. But Rodgers in particular, with his slightly high voice, sounded very folksy. By the sixties, along with the majority of his peers, Rodgers saw his recording career stalled. Regardless, he continued to record and perform. Tragically, all that came to an abrupt end in 1967, when he was brutally attacked—by some accounts, at the hands of an off-duty police officer!—and left for dead with debilitating head injuries. Well over thirty years after the assault (the cause of which was never solved) an acoustic guitar-strumming Rodgers was finally sufficiently recovered to perform again—in Branson, Missouri. (Corbis)

a lil country,

a Li'L rock

RICKY NELSON

opposite: (b. Eric Hilliard Nelson, 5/8/40, Teaneck, N.J., d. 12/31/85) Beginning in 1949 (wow, that far back!) Nelson played himself on radio, and then in 1952, the world watched as he grew up before the public's very eyes. The television show was, of course, *The Adventures of Ozzie and Harriet,* and until it ended its official run in 1966, little Ricky became a member of everyone's family. Considered by most as the "original" teen idol, dreamboat Nelson was certainly an instant pop star once he matured out of adolescence. During the 1956 season, he formed a rock band for one episode. The next year, his rendition of "I'm Walkin'" (the Fats Domino classic) was featured on another singular broadcast. This segment proved so popular with much-needed younger viewers, also making the double-sided release (with "A Teenager's Romance") into a million seller, that all of Nelson's subsequent releases were worked into the program (or tagged on at the end as a separate performance piece). In 1961, he went from "Ricky" to "Rick" to help escape his teenybopper image. Unfortunately, his career was no more immune to the British invasion than any other act, and it was not until 1972 that his career was reinvigorated with the number-one hit "Garden Party." Ironically, Nelson penned that song after receiving a negative reception at a rock revival show; it seems the audience expected its former clean-cut star and was disappointed by his now long-haired, hippyesque appearance. He was the father of actress Tracy Nelson and brothers Matthew and Gunnar, who formed the rock group The Nelsons. (Corbis)

DUANE EDDY

this page: (b. 4/26/38, Corning, N.Y.) Since the age of five, little Eddy played music; his nimble fingers led him to become one of rock and roll's most innovative instrumentalists—and the man many feel most responsible for popularizing the electric guitar. His professional career began after moving to Phoenix, and meeting Lee Hazlewood. (Then a local disc jockey, Hazlewood was setting his sights on producing; he also wrote the Nancy Sinatra hit, "These Boots Are Made for Walking.") Beginning in the mid-fifties, Eddy would eventually record over a dozen Top 40, mainly instrumental, hits. Many of the cuts featured his memorable twangy guitar sound, including "Because They're Young," "Rebel Rouser," and the classic Henry Mancini television theme for "Peter Gunn." From 1962 to 1968, Eddy was married to country singer Jessi Colter ("I'm Not Lisa")—a period in time which saw his influence begin to diminish, but not disappear. In 1986, "Gunn" was revived by The Art of Noise (with Eddy) and won a Grammy as Best Rock Instrumental, a fitting tribute to the man who made "art" from what many others considered only "noise." (Ken Whitmore/MPTV)

this page: (b. Francis Avallone, 9/18/39, Philadelphia, Penn.) A trumpet-playing child prodigy, Avalon made his first recordings in the mid-fifties, which were all instrumentals. A few years later he put to good use what some have called a weak voice and moderate talent, and began releasing pop tunes. Criticism aside, his chart-toppers "Venus" and "Why" quickly made him the most popular teen idol born out of Philly—ahead of Fabian and Bobby Rydell—which was then fairly seething with young talent, thanks to its use as the broadcast base for Dick Clark's *American Bandstand*. However, being one of the baby boomer generation's hottest stars had its downside: underage at the height of his music career, Avalon was not allowed to collect the money he earned—a rather startlingly paltry sum of $100,000 (if measured against today's inflated incomes)—until he turned twenty-one, in 1961. By then, his singing had become secondary to his acting career, which included a string of eight memorable, albeit silly, beach-themed movies (many with fellow music star Annette Funicello). He turns up in a fantasy scene in the movie version of *Grease* (1978) and is rumored to have been one of the stage musical's original investors. The 1980 movie *Idolmaker* is based on his career, that of manager (and talent scout) Robert Manucci, and fellow pretty-boy fave, Fabian. (Corbis)

opposite: (b. Fabian Forte Bonaparte, 2/6/43, Philadelphia, Penn.) Discovered at age fourteen while sitting on his front steps in Philadelphia, Fabian was, if nothing else, the perfect manifestation of the male pin-up. Good-looking in a slightly arrogant, devious way, Fabian had his share of naysayers, to say the least. This sprayed-hair, hypnotic-eyed dreamboat has been unilaterally skewered over the years as nothing more than the skilled creation of management and promotion. Fabian was discovered by Bob Manucci (of Frankie Avalon fame) who was, quite unashamedly, looking for talent to exploit. Manucci groomed fab Fabian as a tamed version of Elvis Presley. A string of appearances on *American Bandstand* made it quickly evident that girls adored him, and, even more notable, guys wanted to be just like him (a teen idol rarity that was cleverly parodied in the 1986 film *Peggy Sue Got Married*). Unfortunately, Fabian's music career faded as quickly as it appeared, sped along by his own revelations about the amount of work necessary to help him vocally in the recording studio. However, Fabian did become quite a credible actor (*North to Alaska*, 1960). By taking advantage of his cunning kisser—nobody looked better on camera—acting allowed him to ride through this rough patch and may have been a far more suitable use of his talent. (Corbis)

POP TOPPERZ

PAUL anka

opposite: (b. 7/30/40, Ottawa, Canada) Anka was yet another musical prodigy. He began writing music at age twelve and burst onto the music scene when his song "Diana" (1957) became an enormous hit (it was reputed to have sold ten million copies worldwide). The tune was about a teen boy in love with a slightly older woman—rather scandalous content at the time. He repeatedly worked quasiserious adolescent relationship themes into his work: "Lonely Boy," "Put Your Head on My Shoulder," and "Puppy Love," which was written about then-steady girlfriend, Annette Funicello (and you thought she was going out with Frankie Avalon, didn't you?!), all to great critical acclaim and even greater chart success. At the peak of his fame (he was a millionaire by age twenty) this Syrian-descended son of restaurant owners moved away from pop and into cabaret-nightclub performing to avoid the hazards encountered by other teen idols; he ended up making more money on the Vegas circuit. Anka also wrote hits for fellow "strip" performers Tom Jones ("She's a Lady") and Frank Sinatra (the English lyrics for "My Way"). His own pop career resurfaced in 1974 with the hit "(You're) Having My Baby"—though he sang the line as "having *our* baby" so he would not offend feminists. Stocky and athletic, he married a former teen model in 1963, and they have been together ever since. Anka also composed the theme for *The Tonight Show, Starring Johnny Carson.* (Corbis)

BOBBY vee

this page: (b. Robert Thomas Velline, 4/30/43, Fargo, N.Dak.) As a young teen, Vee joined his older brother's band, The Shadows, and the group went on to make a name for themselves in the country's great heartland. Their fortunes shifted into high gear by the most bittersweet of circumstances: the band was asked to play in place of Buddy Holly after the singer was killed in his infamous plane crash. In the wake of their successful substitution, the group signed with Liberty Records in the fall of 1959—when Vee was just fifteen! Unfortunately, they did not fare well and the band expected themselves to be dropped from their label, until a disc jockey rescued a B-side ("Devil or Angel") from one of their failed singles. The rereleased record reached number six on the charts. On the strength of his vocals, which were largely given credit for the song's success, Vee secured a solo contract. As a clean-cut, college boy type, Vee had the perfect image for his teen anthem songbook, which included the hits "Take Good Care of My Baby" and "Rubberball." But like many post-Elvis, pre-Beatle acts, his reign as a pop prince lasted only a few short years. Vee did manage some clever pairings with popular "beat" groups—The Crickets and The Ventures—during the mid-sixties, while he was still, for heaven's sake, only in his early twenties! (Hulton-Deutsch/Corbis)

Mark Lindsay

this page: (b. 3/9/42, Cambridge, Idaho). When he was fifteen and working in a bakery—with dreams of music stardom—lanky Lindsay literally took to the stage one night and asked to sing with an unnamed band. So impressed were the boys with Lindsay's singing (and nerve) that the young man was asked to join the group. In 1961, they became Paul Revere and the Raiders, named after their founder, not the Revolutionary War hero. As lead vocalist, saxophonist, and percussionist (he shook a mean tambourine!), the then often pony-tailed Lindsay is credited with producing and cowriting the majority of the group's releases. The band became the first rock group signed to Columbia Records. Naturally, being the front person—in his thigh-high boots and ruffled shirts—he would also become the preferred pinup, among, it should be noted, a group of very good-looking guys. In 1965, the group was asked by Dick Clark to be the "house band" for his new music show *Where the Action Is.* The action lasted for two years, then he and Revere went on to cohost *It's Happening 68.* It certainly was for Lindsay, who, with his charismatic voice and electric onstage persona, was drawing favorable comparisons to Mick Jagger. During the early seventies, mesmerizing Mark had a successful side career as a soloist ("Arizona"), while he and the Raiders had their biggest hit, "Indian Reservation" (1971). In 1975, Lindsay left the group permanently and could be heard singing on a number of commercial jingles for Levi-Strauss, Anheuser-Busch, Nissan, and Baskin-Robbins. (Michael Ochs)

BOBBY SHERMAN

opposite: (b. Robert Cabot Sherman Jr., 7/22/43, Santa Monica, Calif.) Here's a flashback moment: remember those plastic records you could cut out from the back of cereal boxes? Well, here's one artist who featured prominently in that peculiar form of promotion. Times sure have changed! At the end of the sixties, solo male pop stars were on the verge of coming back to the forefront; this sexy, cleft-chin stud was the first teen idol of the dawning decade. Sherman's interest in music started at age eleven, when he learned to play the trumpet—but he also loved to play football. By college age, his fondness for music had outweighed a desire to continue sports. A final decision came when he landed a gig singing on the musical variety series, *Shindig,* lasting two years. In 1968, he got a second big break when he was cast in the series *Here Come the Brides* (alongside another up-and-coming heartthrob, David Soul). This weekly exposure made fans of millions of young women and was the perfect stepping stone for his music career. With his longish hair and exposed chest, decorated with a string of "love" beads or his signature black leather choker (which started a surprise fashion craze among men), he was a dream date come to life. He also became a big, big star. However, four million-sellers and three short years later, one of his biggest hits, "Easy Come, Easy Go" (1971), seemed rather prophetically titled. Sherman's spin on turntables had come to an end. If you can believe it, today this still-handsome singer is a San Bernardino county sheriff and is a specialist in emergency medicine who actively trains cadets in CPR and first aid. (Michael Ochs)

DAViD CaSSiDY

this page: (b. 4/12/50, New York City) The son of actor Jack Cassidy and actress Evelyn Ward, Cassidy became a worldwide sensation when he starred opposite stepmother Shirley Jones on the hit television series *The Partridge Family*. (Notably, he and Jones were the only actual singing members of the TV cast, and Cassidy had no idea that Jones was playing his mother until he was signed on. He also had a long-term affair with actress Susan Dey, who played his sister Laurie—which outlasted the run of the show.) The "group" had a first big hit with "I Think I Love You" (the biggest-selling record of 1970), followed by "I Woke Up in Love this Morning" and Cassidy's solo version of "Cherish." So adored was he at the time that his fan club membership was the largest in history, exceeding those for Elvis and The Beatles. At age twenty-one, he was the highest-paid performer in the world. Cassidy had come very far from his days as a school troublemaker and college dropout. But maybe not: anxious to shed his teen image, he appeared seminude in a *Rolling Stone* magazine feature. The publicity greatly hurt his popularity, and he sank into a three-year "dark" period of alcohol and drug abuse in Los Angeles. Lately, he has taken up theater acting and has played in the shows *Joseph and the Amazing Technicolor Dreamcoat* (you will hear this name again!), *Time*, and *Blood Brothers*, this last one with stepbrother Shaun Cassidy. (Gene Trindl/MPTV)

opposite: (b. 9/27/58, Los Angeles, Calif.) Shaun is the son of actors Jack Cassidy (who certainly had some strong genes and good-looking boys!) and Shirley Jones, and the stepbrother of David Cassidy. When just eleven, slim Shaun sang and composed music with his own band; at sixteen, he signed a record deal (with Warner Bros.) and had a major European hit, "Morning Girl," in 1976. Cast in the television show *The Hardy Boys Mysteries* (1977–79) with Parker Stevenson, Cassidy began his stateside career in earnest. His remake of The Crystals hit "Da Do Ron Ron"—featured on an April 1977 episode—went to number-one. Comely Cassidy is easily one of the most recognized teen idols of his, or any other, age. Yet his popularity far exceeds the expected payoff from such a paltry run at the charts: he had only two more top-ten hits. Though by no means unique, this is evidence that a pretty face can make it seem like you are a bigger star than your talents warrant. But Cassidy had an ace up his sleeve: he became a noted behind-the-scenes television worker, and the series *American Gothic* (1995–96), which he created, wrote, and produced, was a critical, though short-lived, success. (Michael Ochs)

SHaun CaSSiDY

Donny Osmond

(b. 12/9/57, Ogden, Utah) Way back in 1963, when Donny had just turned six, he and his brothers, The Osmonds, debuted on television's *The Andy Williams Show* (the host was a huge early supporter of the group). The act was a hit, but as Osmondmania grew into the seventies, it was obvious who was at the center of attention. With the emergence of the solo teen idol, the boy with the incandescent smile became one of the brightest stars. Osmond's success eclipsed what he shared with his older siblings, making a career out of recycling old pop tunes: "Go Away Little Girl" (originally a hit for Steve Lawrence), "Puppy Love" (Paul Anka), "Too Young" (Nat King Cole), and "The Twelfth of Never" (Johnny Mathis). As the decade progressed, Donny grew out of boyhood cuteness into attractive young manhood, taking with him the adoration of teenage girls all over the world. At his peak, professionally and physically, he perfectly timed his move into a weekly television show, with sister Marie at his side. From 1976 to 1979, the two perky entertainers traded lightweight barbs and sang duets, many of which became hits ("I'm Leavin' It All up to You"). However, when the show ended, an older, now-married Donny found himself without a career; audiences were unwilling to let him grow up. Adding insult to injury, when Osmond starred on Broadway in the 1982 revival of George M. Cohan's *Little Johnny Johns*, the show closed opening night. He took it as a sign that his "star" had been fatally extinguished. For the next few years he stayed off the radar screen, but triumphantly marched back in 1989, with "Soldier of Love." But to this day, he still has difficulty shaking his teen idol image. Poor cutie-pie! (Michael Ochs)

MICHAEL JACKSON

(b. 8/29/58, Gary, Ind.) The self-proclaimed "King of Pop" has spent nearly his entire life as a performer, beginning at age four when he was, unarguably, the main attraction alongside his brothers, The Jackson Five. But being in the spotlight may have been his undoing; onstage, he was confident and exuberant, yet offstage, reclusive and eccentric. His personality "quirks" would become more evident and exploitable as he grew up. Brought to Motown Records, in 1968, by none other than Diana Ross, he and his siblings began scoring hits with "I Want You Back" (1969). But Michael, displaying an enormous amount of vocal maturity and style (his agile moves were patterned after those of legendary James Brown), was an obvious singular sensation. Following his "official" solo debut in 1979, with *Off the Wall* (unofficially, he soloed back in 1971 with "Got to Be There"), Jackson began his monumental assault on the top ranks of pop stardom. The follow-up album, *Thriller*, became the most successful solo recording of all time. For the better part of a decade, with each successive release, commercially Jackson could not miss with the public. But privately, things were entirely another matter. From rumors of aberrant sexual behavior to bizarre goings-on at his ranch, Neverland, it seems that Jackson, who claimed not to have any childhood of his own, was having trouble growing up and reconciling fantasy with reality. Subsequently, the torrent of controversy destabilized the foundation of his success. His latest release, audaciously entitled *Invincible*, was his lowest seller in years and clearly shows that he is not. (Michael Ochs)

GEORGE MICHAEL

opposite: (b. Georgios Yorgos Kyriacos Panayiotou, 6/25/63, London, England) Michael is the son of a Greek restaurateur and English mother. As a young lad, he wanted to be a pilot, but sadly his dream was thwarted by colorblindness. Still, good things lay ahead for Georgie. In 1981, he met Andrew Ridgely. The two became fast friends and formed a band called The Executive. Deep down they knew they were better as a duo, and they reformed as Wham! the following year. The group went on to become the most successful teen-oriented twosome of the decade. But as fast as they arrived, riffs formed in their partnership, caused by the undisclosed fact that Michael's songwriting and performing talent carried the pair. Michael went solo in 1986, "redressed" in black leather, tight torn jeans, aviator sunglasses, and beard stubble. The first release, "I Want Your Sex"—from his landmark album *Faith*—was banned by many radio stations for its adult content. It was followed by four number-one hits—and the album won a Grammy for Album of the Year. His videos also caused a sensation, including his bare butt in "Sex," his in-your-face hip-swiveling in "Faith," and his famous no-show in "Freedom" (1990). Into the mid-nineties, his fortunes changed. In a dispute with then-label Sony, he lost a multimillion-dollar lawsuit in which he charged that they rendered him a "pop slave." Then in 1998, he was arrested in Beverly Hills for "lewd behavior" involving an undercover police officer in a public bathroom. Up until that point, Michael kept his private life to himself, fearing that news of homosexuality would adversely affect his career. The actual amount of harm this revelation may have had on his work is debatable. Very few artists could sustain the level of success that Michael did; by the time of this controversy his star had already shown signs of dimming. (Gary Gershoff/Retna)

RICHARD MARX

this page: (b. 9/16/63, Chicago, Ill.) Marx began his "career" at age five, singing advertising jingles written by his father, including "My dog is bigger than your dog" for Ken-L-Ration. As a more mature professional, he worked as a backup vocalist for Lionel Richie, Kenny Rogers, even Madonna. After this period of apprenticeship, Marx took the plunge and went solo late in the eighties. Almost instantly, with his outrageously poofy hairstyle (à la Tina Turner), he had three successive number-one hits in a row—"Hold on to the Nights," "Satisfied," and "Right Here Waiting" (a tune originally written for Marx's wife, Cynthia Rhodes of Animotion, but one that was slated to be recorded by Barbra Streisand)—and a total of fourteen straight top-twenty singles before the run came to an abrupt end in 1994. A reluctant master at writing the rock "ballad," Marx continues to work now on the producing side of records, listing Vince Gill and *NSYNC among his collaborators. (Kumstedt/Retna)

Har-Men-iZinG

opposite, from left to right: Melvin Franklin (b. David English, 10/12/42, Montgomery, Ala., d. 2/23/95), Paul Williams (b. 7/2/39, Birmingham, Ala., d. 8/17/73), David Ruffin (b. 1/18/41, Meridian, Miss., d. 6/1/91), Otis Williams (b. Otis Miles, 10/30/41, Texarkana, Tex.), and Eddie Kendricks (b. 12/17/39, Union Springs, Ala., d. 10/5/92) The most successful black group in music history formed in Detroit and originally sang as the Elgins, before being renamed by Motown label impresario Berry Gordy in 1961. The astute songwriter and producer Smokey Robinson helped the group early on to establish their unique mix of complex harmonies, featuring Ruffin's baritone and Kendricks's falsetto. "My Girl" was their first chart-topper and a classic example of their hallmark vocal sound. Norman Whitfield "replaced" Robinson in the latter part of the sixties and was instrumental in bringing a rawer edge to their music, reflecting changing times. However, these new dynamics caused both Ruffin (in 1968) and Kendricks (in 1971)—after recording the splendid "Just My Imagination"—to leave the organization. Regardless of the loss, the group's success continued unabated, and their release of "Papa Was a Rolling Stone" (1972) won them their first Grammy—and is considered one of Motown's finest recordings. Despite triumph over the years, four founding members died tragically: Williams, succumbing to alcohol and drug abuse, shot himself in 1973; Ruffin died of a drug overdose in 1991; Kendricks was taken by lung cancer the following year; and Franklin succumbed to heart failure. (Photofest)

four seasons

this page, from left to right: Nick Massi (b. 9/19/35, Newark, N.J., d. 12/24/00), Bob Gaudio (b. 12/17/42, Bronx, N.Y.), Frankie Valli (b. Frankie Castellucio, 5/3/37, Newark, N.J.), and Tommy Devito (b. 6/19/36, Bellville, N.J.) In the mid-fifties, they went by the name The VariaTones, then as The Four Lovers. Valli left the group in 1958 to work as a soloist, rejoining the ensemble in time for their final name selection and the recording of their seminal release "Sherry" in 1962. Noted for splendid orchestrations, Gaudio's clever songwriting, and Valli's memorable falsetto (they were the first group to use the sound as lead instead of back-up), "Sherry" (also their first number-one) along with the follow-ups "Big Girls Don't Cry" and "Walk Like a Man" made the group an undeniable music force. Unexpectedly, their success was repeated with black audiences. Perceived early on by many to be an R&B (nonwhite) group, both "Sherry" and "Girls" topped the soul charts. The group was one of only two in America to hold their own against the British Invasion; thus they were slyly nicknamed "The East Coast Beach Boys." Valli's solo career resurfaced in 1967 with the hit "Can't Take My Eyes off You," and again with "My Eyes Adored You" (1975) and "Grease" (1978). The group itself weathered frequent lineup changes throughout the sixties and seventies, and had two final hits in 1975, "Who Loves You" and "December, 1963." (Photofest)

BANDING TOGETHER

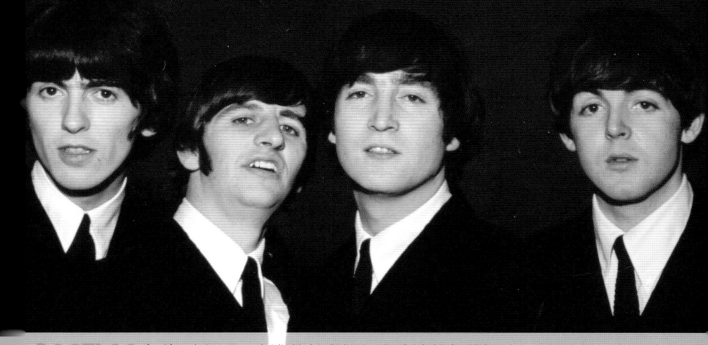

Beatles *from left to right:* George Harrison (b. 2/24/43, d. 11/29/01), Ringo Starr (b. Richard Starkey, 7/7/40), John Lennon (b. 10/9/40, d. 12/8/80), and (James) Paul McCartney (b. 6/18/42); all born Liverpool, England. In the mid-fifties, Lennon formed a band called The Quarrymen. In 1957, he was joined by McCartney and then Harrison, who, at the delicate age of fifteen, became the group's youngest member. (In addition, there was Stu Sutcliffe, bass player, who left in 1961, and drummer Pete Best.) In 1960, they changed their name to The Beatles—in tribute to Buddy Holly's Crickets—and closed ranks with the addition of drummer Starr (who replaced Best) in 1962. Thus, the players in the most influential rock band of all time were cast, the first of *many* culturally significant moments. Another occurred in 1963, with the United Kingdom telecast and subsequent hit status of "Please, Please Me." The song's success signaled the fall (at least for a time) of the solo singer and the rise of the "beat" group (so-called for their music's constant rhythmic and percussive undertones). Another moment took place when the "boys" began dominating domestic (and worldwide) charts, and became the first British act to make such an important and lasting impression. The Beatles also changed the way music was generally produced by preferring to pen their own material, rather than record nonoriginal compositions. (Notably, Lennon and McCartney are widely considered music's greatest pop composers.) They were also the first band members to became movie stars, with the semiautobiographical film *A Hard Day's Night* (1964). (Note: in the classic 1968 animated feature, *Yellow Submarine*, their speaking voices were dubbed.) The band can lay claim to one long list of superlatives after another (including a record nineteen number-one singles), and their success and influence would well outlast their own parting. Almost exactly twenty years after the group's separation, in 1970, the release of the 2000 compilation CD, *1s*, became one of the biggest-selling albums of their entire career. (Michael Ochs)

from left to right: Dennis Wilson (b. 12/4/44, Hawthorne, Calif., d. 12/28/83), Brian Wilson (b. 6/20/42, Hawthorne, Calif.), Mike Love (b. 3/15/41, Baldwin Hills, Calif.), Al Jardine (b. 9/3/42, Lima, Ohio), and Carl Wilson (b. 12/21/46, Hawthorne, Calif., d. 2/6/98) Formed with three brothers, a cousin, and one schoolmate, and managed by Murray Wilson (father to Brian, Carl, and Dennis), The Beach Boys became the most successful and compelling group in American rock history. Unwittingly, lead songwriter Brian—credited with creating their signature "California" sound—saw his personal affairs become the most publicized. His childhood of reputed physical and mental abuse at the hands of his father (a onetime performing hopeful) made him painfully susceptible to the rigorous demands and harsh glare of stardom. At the height of the group's fame, Brian experienced two nervous breakdowns and became addicted to barbituates (however, he was far from the only band member to succumb), which forced him to temporarily retire from performing. During his absence, he was replaced by singer Glen Campbell. Unfortunately, his illnesses led to a general deterioration of his overall health—from which he has never fully recovered. Over the years, the band itself has weathered more than its fair share of life-threatening jolts and performed with a variety of different personnel lineups. This has caused hostile feelings among original members and resulted in a number of lawsuits filed for ownership of the actual name and music. Once viewed as the only substantial rivals to The Beatles, they were voted the number-one group in the world in 1966. Late that same year, they also released what is regarded as their finest recording, "Good Vibrations." Although from a technical standpoint their work is considered relatively benign, collectively and individually each member has contributed to an undeniably important musical and cultural legacy. (Hulton-Deutsch/Corbis)

BEACH BOYS

Dave Clark 5

from left to right: Denis Payton (b. 8/11/43, London, England), Rick Huxley (b. 8/5/42, Dartford, Kent, England), Dave Clark (b. 12/15/42, London, England), Lenny Davidson (b. 5/30/44, Enfield, Middlesex, England), and Mike Smith (b. 12/6/43, London, England) Hunky Clark was a film stuntman and extra before turning to a musical career way back in 1958, when he united his handsome group of merry men as a backing band for a London singer named Stan Saxon; they were formally introduced in 1962. Underrated and overshadowed by fellow British acts, they still had a distinctive sound. Smith, incidentally, sang lead vocals, while Clark played the drums—best heard on their number-one hit "Over and Over" and "I Like It like That" (both 1965). They appeared on *The Ed Sullivan Show* more times than any other British act. Sullivan was said to have really liked them, and as cute as they were, obviously so did the audience! Breaking up in 1971, Clark, a savvy businessman, went on to become quite wealthy (he also cowrote and produced the hit 1986 London stage musical *Time*). Other members went on to less-publicized public and private endeavors. (Michael Ochs)

from left to right: Karl Green (b. 7/31/47, Manchester, England), Barry Whitwam (b. 7/21/46, Manchester, England), Peter Noone (b. 11/5/47, Manchester, England), Keith Hopwood (b. 10/26/46, Manchester, England), and "Lek" (Derek) Leckenby (b. 5/14/45, Leeds, England, d. 6/4/94) As The Heartbeats, they hardly registered on the monitor; as Herman's Hermits, they became the closest native competitors of The Beatles—with early sales of nearly ten million records! Named after the *Rocky and Bullwinkle* character Sherman (whom Peter Noone was said to have resembled) and a rhyme about "Herman the Hermit," this group over the short course of two years gave the world the idiosyncratic hits, "I'm into Something Good," "Mrs. Brown You've Got a Lovely Daughter," and "I'm Henry the VII, I Am." They were considered the "safe" face of beat music, and Noone in particular—whom everyone assumed was named Herman—was the safest and most popular in the bunch. Interestingly, though they were darlings of American teens, the English press looked down on them, considering them too lightweight—especially in comparison to you-know-who. However, it was with the rise of The Monkees that their success waned; it seemed public tastes could only handle one nutty musical group at a time. Their last major chart hit, "There's a Kind of Hush" (1967), was a significantly pleasant style departure from earlier releases. By the advent of psychedelic rock in the late sixties though, as too-wholesome relics of music's own recent past, they were gone in a puff of colored smoke. (Michael Ochs)

HERMAN'S HERMITS

monkees

clockwise, from left to right: Mickey Dolenz (b. 3/8/45, Tarzana, Calif.), (Robert) Michael Nesmith (b. 12/30/42, Houston, Tex.), Peter Tork (b. Peter Halsten Thorkelson, 2/13/42, Washington, D.C.), and Davy Jones (b. 12/30/45, Manchester, England) In 1965, producers Bob Rafelson and Bert Schneider proposed a TV show that focused on the life of a struggling band; the network (ABC) loved the idea. However, existing acts, like the Lovin' Spoonful, proved unsuitable, so auditions were held for outside applicants. Eventually, two musicians, Nesmith and Tork, were teamed with a pair of up-and-coming actor-singers, Jones and Dolenz. Airing in September of 1966, the show received initial ratings that were quite low, but a huge following soon developed. Two singles—"I'm a Believer" (written by Neil Diamond) and "Last Train to Clarksville"—along with a debut album were instant million sellers. But adverse publicity concerning member participation on recordings caused problems. The truth was that their songs were recorded by another group; The Monkees simply overdubbed the vocals. Amidst the controversy, the band continued to release hit material: "Pleasant Valley Sunday" and "Daydream Believer." A third album—*Headquarters*—did feature the "real" band, but the end was now in sight. Tork left in 1968, Nesmith shortly thereafter. As cultural phenomenons go, they lasted a relatively long time, and aside from all the criticism, the group was responsible for some of the best American pop of the period. Some trivia: Nesmith's 1981 video "Elephant Parts" was the first to win a Grammy and he has been credited with being a major early developer of MTV; Jones received a Tony award nomination for the original role of "The Artful Dodger" in the musical, *Oliver!* (Gene Trindl/MPTV)

from left to right: Alan Longmuir (b. 6/20/51), Eric Faulkner (b. 10/21/55), Les McKeown (b. 11/12/55), Stuart "Woody" Wood (b. 2/25/57), and Derek Longmuir (b. 3/19/53); all born Edinburgh, Scotland. A full decade after The Beatles, another United Kingdom group (this time from Scotland) caused enormous waves on the music scene—although it was reduced to a ripple in a relative short amount of time. This go-round, instead of sharp suits, skinny ties, and pointy shoes, they were dressed in revealingly open plaid shirts (an especially apt fashion choice for the well-developed hairy torso of McKeown), tartan knickers, and brightly colored sneakers paired with striped sweatsocks (another disarming style selection, this one best seen on the meaty calves of Derek Longmuir). All rather pretty stuff, huh?! The year 1975 proved their most successful year, with a number of British hits and the American pop chart number-one anthem "Saturday Night." The group officially disbanded in 1978, though several members kept together as The Rollers, then as The New Rollers. (The original name came from the random selection of a spot on the map: Bay City, Michigan.) Unfortunately, over the course of the next few years some of those remaining members became embroiled in controversy: McKeown struck and killed a seventy-five-year-old widow with his car and was charged with reckless driving; Faulkner and (Alan) Longmuir attempted suicide; and manager Tam Paton was jailed on charges of indecent acts with minors. So much for their sweet and wholesome image! Though for many the popularity of the "BCR" falls into the category of "what were we thinking?", one cannot underestimate how massive it once was, and to this day they have a large cult following in the United Kingdom, Germany, and Japan. (Gunther/MPTV)

Bay City Rollers

95

spandau ballet

clockwise, from top left: Martin Kemp (b. 10/10/61), Tony Hadley (b. 6/2/60), Gary Kemp (b. 10/16/59), John Keeble (b. 7/5/59), and Steve Norman (b. 3/25/60) (all born London, England). With a name inspired by an inscription outside a Berlin prison, this group was made up of five schoolmates masterminded by (Gary) Kemp. Spandau Ballet was considered one of the first "new romantic" groups to come out of the late-seventies London fashion scene. The band members were notably attractive and wore blush, eye makeup, and pretty (sometimes downright feminine) clothes. Their music was considered escapist (a counterpoint to punk, which was politically motivated, though both were trends borne of the English working class). Imposing and handsome, six-foot-four Hadley was thrust into the forefront as lead singer, while the rest of the members suffered no less in their backup positions, with each enjoying their own sizeable fan base. Of their two biggest American hits "Gold" and "True" the latter has become a classic mid-eighties slow dance ballad. Before the group dissolved, the two Kemp brothers found acclaim in acting: they both appeared in the *The Krays,* and Gary in *The Bodyguard.* Sadly, after their parting, Hadley, Keeble, and Norman sued unsuccessfully to share in songwriting royalties. (Michael Putland/Retna)

clockwise, from top left: Andy Taylor (b. 2/16/61, Wolverhampton, England), Roger Taylor (b. 4/26/60, Birmingham, England), (Nigel) John Taylor (b. 6/20/60, Birmingham, England), Nick Rhodes (b. Nicholas Bates, 6/8/62, Birmingham, England), and Simon LeBon (b. 10/27/58, Bushey, Hertsfordshire, England) This group of spiky-haired fops took their name from a character in the 1968 cult film *Barbarella* and are truly the only British group to perform in America whose popularity came anywhere close to that of The Beatles (them again!) decades earlier. Kings of the synthesized pop tune and forerunners of the video generation—their first major release, "Girls on Film," featured scantily clad *Penthouse* models and was initially banned from MTV—Duran was very much a "new romantic" band in the beginning before progressing to something closer to white funk. They were a considerably talented group of songwriters, and in later years maintained a career of much higher heights and longevity than their peers. Even when Roger Taylor and Andy Taylor left in the late eighties to pursue other interests, remaining members LeBon, Rhodes, and John Taylor successfully conjured up "Ordinary World" and "Come Undone." Though all of the members became teen idols, lead singer LeBon greatly enhanced his heartthrob status by marrying supermodel Yasmine Parvenah. (Janette Beckman/Retna)

Duran Duran

new edition

below, from left to right: Johnny Gill, a member beginning in 1986 (b. 5/22/66, Washington, D.C.), Ralph Tresvant (b. 5/16/68, Roxbury, Mass.), Michael Bivins (b. 8/10/68, Roxbury, Mass.), Bobby Brown (b. 2/5/69, Boston, Mass.), Ricky Bell (b. 9/18/67, Roxbury, Mass.), and Ronnie DeVoe (b. 11/17/67, Roxbury, Mass.) Officially, this group began in the late seventies, when Bell (one of eleven children), Bivins, and Brown (the group's bad boy) joined forces and appeared in minor talent shows around Boston, until they were taken under the wing of "discoverer" Maurice Starr. As their manager, Starr secured a record deal and loosely patterned his young charges (now a quintet) after the Jackson Five. However, it took them two years to release product, and the result, the obviously Jackson-influenced "Candy Girl" was not well received by their label. Nevertheless, it fared quite well with the public—the first of many hits— but its success forced a label change and the ousting of Starr (who went elsewhere). Credited as the "father" of boy-bands, New Edition lasted longer than many of their "offspring" by growing musically from candied pop to hip-hop. Their latent sound, also called "new jack swing" set the beat for the nineties and helped individual members, Brown in particular, retain high profile careers once they separated from the group. (Steve Granitz/Retna)

opposite, from left to right: Donald Wahlberg (b. 8/17/69, Boston, Mass.), Daniel Wood (b. 5/14/69, Boston, Mass.), Jordan Knight (b. 5/17/70, Worchester, Mass.), Jonathan Knight (b. 11/29/68, Worchester, Mass.), and Joe(y) McIntyre (b. 12/31/72, Needham, Mass.) First formed back in 1984, this Beantown quintet was discovered by New Edition manager Maurice Starr, who just so happened to be looking for a white counterpart to his most recent successful charges. Named after a lyric in a rap song (offered up by Starr), the boys and their self-titled first album were instantly and incredibly popular. In the summer of 1988, they had their first chart hit, "Please Don't Go Girl," followed by nine top-twenty entries, including three number-ones. One major reason for their success was a relatively simple concept: each "kid" in the group appealed to a different potential audience member, theoretically increasing the overall number of fans. Their amazing popularity was evidence that, like it or not, the idea works—at least for a time. But, as expected, things began to peter out in 1992. By then, they had abbreviated their name to NKOTB, in the hopes that this, along with a newer sound, would keep them in good stead with listeners. However, as is almost always the case in these matters, their audience was maturing and moving on, along with likely new converts. They officially split up in 1994 to pursue separate interests: Wahlberg (brother of Mark) went into acting, and both Knight and McIntyre released solo recordings. (Neal Preston/Corbis)

new kids on the block

color me badd

from left to right: Mark Calderon (b. 9/27/70), Bryan Abrams (b. 11/16/69), Sam Watters (b. 7/23/70), and Kevin Thornton (b. 6/17/69); all born Oklahoma City, Okla. If the idea of gathering together different physical types of one race into a musical group increases your chances of reaching a larger audience, then does the combination of different ethnicities make your chances even better? That type of reasoning certainly played a hand in the success of this group. Color Me Badd began singing together in an Oklahoma City high school in the mid-eighties. They were aggressive and talented but lacked the proper management that could set them on the road to fame and fortune. Then one day, Robert "Kool" Bell (of Kool and the Gang) was passing through town on tour and by chance heard them singing. (Truth be told, the guys made it their mission to sing privately for Mr. Bell backstage.) Impressed by what he heard, he hooked them up with his New York City managers. Voilà! Well, not *that* fast; they lived a year in "The Big Apple" before they were able to secure a record deal. Originally they had the name Take One, but it was changed to avoid confusion with the group Take 6. In early 1991, the release of their single "I Wanna Sex You Up" became one of the biggest songs of the year, and due to its risqué content, the most controversial. They followed up with a pair of number-ones: "I Adore Mi Amor" and "All 4 Love." Unfortunately, the adult content of their music was also their downfall; the foursome seemed awkward, often appearing rather silly, singing prurient verse. (It didn't help matters that they were styled in coordinated candy-colored suits!) By 1998, after a number of years of chart inactivity, the group officially parted and on rather unfriendly terms. Abrams continues his music career, as does Watters, but both Calderon and Thornton have chosen a more private course. (Pete Tangen/Retna)

clockwise, from top left: Mark Anthony Owen (b. 1/27/74, Manchester, England), Gary Barlow (b. 1/20/71, Frodsham, Cheshire, England), Jason Thomas Orange (b. 7/10/70, Manchester, England), Howard Paul Donald (b. 4/28/68, Manchester, England), and Robbie Williams (b. 2/13/74, Port Wale, England) In their native England, this vocal group came the closest to emulating the popularity of The Beatles, and were, arguably, the first in this latest wave of boy-band acts (if your memory only allows you to include the Backstreet Boys, *NSYNC, et al.). So, too, their single "Back for Good" (1995) is considered the first charting American hit from this same wave. Before aligning as Take That, Barlow (a songwriter), Owens (a soccer player), and Williams (an aspiring actor) were with a group called, if you can believe the audacity, Cutest Rush—although there is little disputing the fact that they were just that. Once together with Orange and Donald (both dancers) they released their debut album in 1991. They quickly attracted attention for their catchy pop tunes, dance moves, questionable clothes and hairstyles, and yes, good looks. Pretty boys doesn't even come close to describing them! Williams abruptly departed in 1995 and has gone on to solo success—due, in no small part, to a sizeable number of gay fans who follow along this sinewy lad's propensity to cavort around on video and pose for magazines in the nude! The group itself totally disbanded in 1996. Despite their remarkable United Kingdom success—which includes an astounding eight number-one singles—they never had the same impact on the American market (with the exception of "Back"). This left the door open for domestic acts to walk right in, and the masses were not long in coming. (Lenny Baker/Retna)

Take That

BACKSTREET BOYS

They formed in Orlando, Florida, taking their name from a popular flea market in the area, and gave their first live performance at Sea World in 1993. At the time American record buyers were into alternative rock and "gangsta" rap (which, by the way, are still popular today), and definitely not into the group's brand of light pop. It was decided that they should move to Europe, where, because young audiences continued to favor such frivolous fare, it would be considerably easier for them to establish their music career. (It was markedly cheaper, too!) Germany was the first country to take a shine to them, and by the time of their American "relaunch" in 1997, they were household names on the entire continent. Time to set sail back to the states. Seemingly overnight, their smashing domestic success—starting with "Quit Playing Games (with My Heart)"—changed the course of American popular culture. Never before had the record-buying public turned out in such numbers; they snapped up albums in astonishing amounts and did it faster than ever before in chart history. The Boys' popularity opened the gates for a host of imitators, of varying degrees of talent, and the music marketplace became a parade of pre- and postpubescent pretty boys. (Bill Davila/Retna)

opposite, from left to right: Groomed as "successors" to the United Kingdom group Boyzone (in much the same way that *NSYNC followed the Backstreet Boys), this unique Irish fivesome—disputably the cutest of them all—continues the successful ways of boy-bands into the twenty-first century. Egan, Filan, and Feehily met while performing in a local production of *Grease* and with three other lads formed a group called IOU. When this latter trio was replaced by Byrne (a soccer player) and McFadden, the official Westlife lineup was established. *Luverly!* Though they may be *too* much eye candy for some (although you'd have to be quite jaded not to give them a glance or two), with seven consecutive English chart number-ones and counting, they certainly don't lack merit. Surprisingly, they have yet to make a significant impact on the American market (an ongoing problem for all comparable British boy-band acts). Likely because we are so saturated with our own native "sons"—and, in actuality, the "wave" has crested on both sides of the Atlantic—no official attempt has been made or is planned. For the time being it seems that these little hotties will remain where they are and fans will have to go to them. (Michael Brennan/Corbis)

WESTLiFE

Paul nicholas

this page: (b. Paul Beuselinck, 12/3/45, Peterborough, England) Of all the categories of popular music, dance (or disco) is largely dominated by female talent. Nevertheless, a rogue male or two will step onto the dance floor and into the spotlight. Nicholas was one of those gents and had a major million-selling boogie-night hit with "Heaven on the 7th Floor" (1977). Smartly, since his music career never got much higher, he became an actor (and eventual producer) to pay the bills when the elevator came back down. (Michael Ochs)

opposite: (b. Harry Wayne Casey, **KC** 1/31/51, Hialeah, Fla.) Casey was brought up on gospel music, while his mother and aunt sang on local television commercials. At age seventeen, he worked menial tasks at TK Records in Miami, just so that he could get a chance to work in music. Learning from the ground up, he and bass player Richard Finch eventually wrote, produced, arranged, and performed on all their dance funk hit singles (which includes one of the defining dance singles of the era, "Rock Your Baby," written for George Macrae). Culturally, the Sunshine Band is also significant in that it was one of the most popular racially integrated acts in music. The group's first hit "Get Down Tonight" (1975), featuring a unique and revolutionary sped-up guitar track, revolutionized the sound of dance music. Though it was one of five number-one hits, his music was considered nonprogressive (an antidisco sentiment, to be sure). In retrospect this man's work is far more progressive, albeit deceptively simple, than it has ever been given credit and, thanks to retro-music nostalgia, is enjoying a much-deserved renaissance in popularity. (David Redfern/Retna)

DancinG KinGz

milli vanilli

from top to bottom: Fabrice Morvan (b. 5/14/66) and Rob Pilatus (b. 6/8/65, New York City, d. 4/2/98) Pilatus was brought up in an orphanage; Morvan had high hopes of being a trampoline performer until a neck injury made it too dangerous to continue. The two became dancers with various German troupes before forming the infamous duo (named for a defunct New York club) under the auspices of producer Frank Farian. With their model-handsome faces, tight bodies squeezed into spandex, and flamboyant rasta-styled hair, they sashayed onto the music scene with a quartet of international hits, including "Girl I'm Gonna Miss You" and "Blame It on The Rain." Their startling popularity swept over into the established music community too, and they were awarded with the 1989 Grammy as Best New Artist among other accolades. However, it was quickly discovered that neither gentleman actually sang on their recordings (though with those legs it is quite obvious they did the dancing!), and, under the circumstances, it became necessary for them to return their prize. This was hardly the first time records were made in this manner, but a troublesome indication that we were entering into a new period in the industry, thanks to video, where it was okay if you didn't sound the part so long as you looked it. However, since it was the highest profile incident of this nature, organizations wanted to send out a signal to all would-be illusionists. Pilatus's death from a drug overdose is directly attributed to the shame brought on by this controversy. (Neal Preston/Corbis)

from left to right: Randy Jones (The Cowboy, b. 9/13/52, New York City), David Hodo (The Construction Worker, b. 7/7/57, San Andreas, Calif.), Felipe Rose (The Indian, b. 1/22/55, New York City), Victor Willis (The Policeman, b. 7/7/51, Dallas, Tex.), Glenn Hughes (The Leatherman, b. 7/8/50, Bronx, N.Y., d. 3/4/01), and Alexander Briley (The Serviceman, b. 4/12/51, New York City) After watching Rose perform (in Indian costume) on a street in New York City's Greenwich Village, record producer Jacque Morali came up with the idea to form an entire music group composed of gay "macho" male icons. Assembled in 1977, Morali secured a contract with Casablanca and gathered together songs deliberately written with (some might say covert, others overt) gay content. They first charted in the United Kingdom with "San Francisco," then the United States with "Macho Man" (1978), and were especially popular in underground gay clubs (*quelle surprise!*). But gay fans tired of the group the more popular they became with the straight mainstream ("YMCA" and "In the Navy"). With the coming eighties and a disco backlash, their fortunes slipped measureably. In vain, they attempted a relaunch as a "new romantic" group—makeup, satin, high hair, etc.—but the conversion met with no success. Both Morali and Hughes died of AIDS-related illnesses, but the group continues on as a vital part of the nostalgia market. Though criticized as nothing more than a "concept" act, they did put a face on what was being called "faceless music," and became the genre's most recognizable act. (Michael Ochs)

ViLLAGe PeOPLe

PAT Boone

opposite: (b. Charles Eugene Patrick Boone, b. 6/1/34, Jacksonville, Fla.) Though a definitive teen idol and one who was surprisingly sexy, Boone had a squeaky clean image—enhanced by white buck shoes and immaculately pomaded hair. He was groomed to be in direct contrast to his recording contemporaries. Therein lay his strength: he was the most popular late-fifties recording artist, just after rival Elvis Presley. Hits began with tame "white" versions of R&B songs ("Ain't That a Shame"), then ballads ("Love Letters in the Sand") toward the end of the decade. Boone was also a success as husband: he nixed a role in which he was supposed to kiss Marilyn Monroe (the film, *Bus Stop*) because the actress was not his wife. He married in 1953 to Shirley Foley (daughter of country singer Red Foley), and the happy couple had four little girls in quick succession (including daughter Debby, who went on to record the single "You Light Up My Life," the top song of 1977). He also continued in college during the height of his career, eventually graduating from Columbia. Boone also had his own television show from 1957–60 and wrote several "inspirational" best-selling books for teens. But even his popularity could not withstand the cultural changes that came with the sixties. He floundered until turning to gospel music in the late sixties, where he has more or less stayed with one notable exception. In the mid-nineties he shocked fans by releasing a heavy metal album. In addition, for a politically conservative man in his early sixties, he appeared to have no qualms appearing shirtless for all the world to see to announce its release. In his defense, the body wasn't half bad for a guy his age! (Corbis)

this page: (b. Billy Joe Thomas, 8/7/42, Hugo, Okla.) Thomas was raised in Houston **B. J. Thomas** and sang in church as a child. As a teen, he joined a local rock band, The Triumphs, and became their lead singer. In the late sixties, he went solo, and had hits with "Hooked on a Feeling" and the classic "Raindrops Keep Fallin' on My Head" (the 1969 Oscar-winning song from *Butch Cassidy and the Sundance Kid* and Thomas's first number-one). In the early seventies, he began recording religious music, while still releasing the occasional hit like "(Hey Won't You Play) Another Somebody Done Somebody Wrong Song" (his second number-one). In the eighties, now as a full-fledged born-again Christian, Thomas admitted to years of alcohol and drug abuse—and was on the road to recovery. (Michael Ochs)

Isaac Hayes

(b. 8/20/42, Covington, Tenn.) Hayes moved to Memphis as a young man and found work writing songs. With David Porter, he was responsible for penning the R&B masterpieces "Hold On, I'm Comin'" and "Soul Man," but he was not happy as a behind-the-scenes player. Capitalizing on a flair for lavishly orchestrated pieces and a memorable stage look that consisted of heavy gold chains, brightly colored tights and boots—a bare-chested, gleamingly bald-pated, and sweating Hayes rode high during the late sixties and early seventies—peaking with his erotic dance classic "(Theme from) Shaft" in 1971. Though his "act" would eventually dissolve into almost self-parody, when he performed on the 1972 Oscar telecast, the unapologetic sensual black male had *finally* arrived. Understandably, the segment is considered an important piece of cultural history and not to be missed if you have the chance to view it. (Incidentally, the composition won the Academy Award for Best Song of the Year.) Hayes reinvigorated his career of late by lending his voice to the Chef character on the TV comedy cult fave, *South Park*. However, this former "Black Messiah" who was raised by his grandmother now shows up for work *with* his shirt on. (Gunther/Retna)

TEDDY PENDERGRASS

(b. 3/26/50, Philadelphia, Pa.) As the onetime lead singer for Harold Melvin and the Blue Notes (from 1970–76), Pendergrass used his distinctive and sensual vocals to make memorable classics out of the hits "If You Don't Know Me by Now," "The Love I Lost," and "Wake Up, Everybody." The vocals also made the man a standout attraction with the ladies! Conflicts with Melvin led to his inevitable departure, whereby he launched a successful solo career. "Teddy Bear" (as he became known to fans) embarked on a series of super sexy late-seventies concerts with the title "Ladies Only" and was the unrivaled soul singer supreme of the slow, romantic R&B love song. His professional and private life was in full swing when a tragic 1982 auto accident—that included some scandalous and unverifiable details involving a transgendered passenger—left him paralyzed from the waist down. Thankfully his voice remained intact, and though he was confined to a wheelchair successful therapy was able to help him continue performing. Pendergrass was ordained a minister when only age ten, and he credits his deep faith with getting him through this harrowing ordeal. (Neal Preston/Corbis)

111

al Green

opposite: (b. 4/13/46, Forrest City, Ark.) Green began recording in 1960, but didn't have his breakthrough until 1971, with the release of "Tired of Being Alone" and his masterpiece "Let's Stay Together." For the next few years he dominated R&B music with his energetic presence and titillating sexual manner. Ironically, this quintessential soul man was ordained as a minister in 1976. Although he always cherished his gospel roots, an unfortunate incident with onetime girlfriend Mary Woodson set him, for a time, totally on the path of righteousness. The story goes that following an argument between the two, Woodson burned Green in his bathtub with scalding water, then shot and killed herself. At the time, Green was already disenchanted with the recording industry, so he ended his contract and formed his own label, American Music. He still continued to release secular work until a stage fall in 1979—which he swore was a sign from God—convinced him to devote his work to religion. In 1983, his first all-gospel album appeared, and his ministry, The Full Gospel Tabernacle in Memphis, is where you can find this 1995 Rock and Roll Hall of Fame inductee singing today. (Since the late eighties, Green has still been known to sneak off occasionally to record mainstream.) (Michael Ochs)

this page: (b. 10/7/57, Kenova, W. Va.) After high school, Smith had attended college for only one semester before he was led astray by drugs and alcohol. His addiction eventually caused a complete physical and mental breakdown. By 1979, he rehabilitated himself as a born-again Christian, then moved to Nashville in the hopes of becoming a songwriter. In 1982, he landed a job as keyboardist with singer Amy Grant's band and the following year released his solo album. For angelic and adorable Smith, it was an instant hit. Since then he has become one of contemporary Christian music's most successful and rewarded performers. He has had two major pop hits, "Place in this World" and "I Will Be Here for You," and he has won Grammys and countless Dove awards (given by The Gospel Music Association). He is also a best-selling author. Although he has cut back his workload in recent years to devote time to his family, this bewitchingly blue-eyed singer gives God complete credit for his writing and singing talent, but, unquestionably, he owes a lot of his popularity to being one of the "Most Beautiful People in America" (*People* magazine, 1992). (Beth Gwinn/Retna)

michael W. Smith

opposite, from left to right: Scott Stapp (b. 8/8/73, Orlando, Fla.), Scott Phillips (b. 2/22/73, Madison, Fla.) and Mark Tremonti (b. 2/18/75, Detroit, Mich.) Founder Stapp was brought up with such strict religious beliefs (which forbade the playing of rock music) that he ran away from home at age seventeen. For a time, he and Tremonti went to the same high school, in Orlando, Florida, before Stapp—with the intention of becoming a lawyer—attended college at Florida State University in Tallahassee. A huge Doors fan, he was impressed to learn that lead singer Jim Morrison had once lived in the same city. The knowledge inspired Stapp, no longer a student, to form his own rock band with Tremonti. Creed debuted in 1998 and quickly became known as a back-to-rock band, with definite, though somewhat elusive, religious undertones to their work. With their single, "Arms Wide Open" they gained international recognition, a number-one spot, and Grammy for Best Rock Song of 2000, embracing hordes of converts. Stapp, who has a vocal sound reminiscent of Pearl Jam's Eddie Vedder, considers the music they record as his new religion; critics label it "born-again" rock; and fans of this tasty trio believe the guys are definitely heaven-sent. (John McMurtrie/Retna)

BOYZ II men

this page, from top left to right: Wanya "Squirt" Morris (b. 7/29/73), Michael "Bass" McCary (b. 12/16/72), Nathan "Alex Vanderpool" Morris (b. 6/18/71), and Shawn "Slim" Stockman (b. 9/26/72); all born Philadelphia, Pa. When all four met at the Philadelphia High School of Creative and Performing Arts in the late eighties, they had a great deal in common. They were mainly poor; they sought solace in the church; they considered their mothers as their strongest role models; and they were encouraged early in life to sing. Originally, there were five members in the group, but the fifth unlucky member decided to go solo right before their big break! In 1988, Michael Bivins (of New Edition and recently Bell, Biv, Devoe) brought them to Motown. By 1991, with the release of their first hit, aptly titled "Motownphilly," they were fast on their way to becoming the most successful group of the nineties. To date, they have the record for the most weeks at number-one—sixteen—for "One Sweet Day" (a distinction they shared with collaborator Mariah Carey). Amazingly, two of their earlier songs, "End of the Road" and "I'll Make Love to You," held the two previous records. Despite their astonishing success, it is not surprising to learn that they are deemed too sweet for a current marketplace inundated with sexually explicit music and musicians. (Steve Granitz/Retna)

this page: (b. 3/5/58, Manchester, England, d. 3/10/88) His mother was a singer and his father a drummer and big band leader, but little Andy is best known as the baby brother of the enormously successful male trio, The Bee Gees. Slim, muscular, all white teeth and hair, and by far the cutest sibling (alright, a young teenage Maurice was quite a looker, too), Gibb became a superstar in his own right at just nineteen with an astounding triplet of consecutive number-one songs, "I Just Want to Be Your Everything," "Love Is Thicker han Water," and "Shadow Dancing." He even eclipsed, for a time, his own brothers (who were, not so incidentally, responsible for furnishing his material). However, by 1980, his popularity plummeted, due likely to his association with disco-pop. (Nothing can kill a music career faster than recording in a genre that is passé!) He turned to other endeavors as his star declined, including a stint on television as cohost of *Solid Gold.* Having amassed a fortune in his heyday, he consoled himself through this downturn with partying; unfortunately, he also developed a dangerous dependence on cocaine. During this time, he was in a long-term relationship with actress Victoria Principal (*Dallas*), but their breakup only led to more drug use. By the late eighties, with his money squandered and health suffering irreparably, Gibb died of an inflammatory heart virus. Gibb has a daughter named Peta, from a short-lived marriage, whom he had only seen once before passing away. (Lynn Goldsmith/Corbis)

opposite: (b. Elvis Aron Presley, 1/18/35, Tupelo, Miss., d. 8/16/77) **ELViS PReSLEY**

If one star's popularity could set the standards for others to emulate, then that celebrity would be Presley. Devoted fans made him into a legend, and they had been with him since the beginning, when he was known as "The Hillbilly Cat" and first recorded for Sun Records in 1954. His fans then gave him seventeen number-one songs, from his first, "Heartbreak Hotel" (1956), to his last, "Suspicious Minds" (1969). In between they bought over six hundred million pieces of vinyl. They bided their time through his army enlistment, which inspired the musical *Bye, Bye Birdie.* Followers queued in line, from 1956 until 1969, to view his barely watchable roster of thirty-three films (and didn't seem to mind that acting may have marred the integrity of his music work). They *glimpsed* him on the historic *Ed Sullivan Show* broadcast in 1956 and his comeback concert in 1968, and they *watched* as he sang "Aloha from Hawaii via Satellite" in 1973. They swooned over a slim and sexy Presley and endured a paunchy Presley (in sparkly outfits inspired by good friend Liberace). And in the end, devotees visited his home and final resting place, Graceland, making it a pop culture Mecca. Yes, devoted to him they were, like he was to his own mother Gladys. And to them in return he was devoted with a notorious generosity, sometimes buying a fan a car or two. If they had known him when he was just a movie theater usher, or truck driver (with blond hair), they probably would have also been at his side. They are still there, in numbers too great to count, listening, watching, and waiting for his expected return. Now that's what I'd call some kind of a fan! (Kobal)

opposite: (b. James Douglas Morrison, 12/8/43, Melbourne, Fla. d. 7/3/71) He was a cultural icon of the promises and excesses of the sixties. Starting very young, Morrison began writing poetry as a way to escape his already troubled life (for a time he was so estranged from his parents, he claimed them to be dead). When Morrison was old enough he moved to Los Angeles and enrolled into (and graduated from) the Theatre Arts School of UCLA. But instead of becoming part of the work force when he finished college, he fell in with hippies, drugs, and alcohol. However, within this hazy, hash-filled world, the still poetic Morrison stumbled upon former classmate Ray Manzarek, who was then with a struggling band. Manzarek became enthralled with Morrison's poetry and suggested his words be set to music. They joined forces, named their group The Doors (inspired by a William Blake poem), and laid seige upon the music world. Their very first hit (after the group gained a favorable reputation performing at L.A.'s famed Whiskey-A-Go-Go) was the landmark "Light My Fire" (1967). The song, skillfully combining eroticism with death, won them international acclaim. Their newfound success did not sit well with Morrison, who wanted acceptance only as a serious musician. Circumstances were exacerbated by Morrison's growing popularity as a sex symbol (which he did little to dissuade with his highly sensualized performances) and continual substance abuse. Ultimately, his bad behavior created insurmountable problems. The Doors lost bookings and money, and Morrison was threatened with jail for indecent exposure. At the thought of prison, he and girlfriend Pamela Courson fled to Paris. There, things caught up with him; he died of a heart attack brought on by his addictions. News of Morrison's death was withheld for over a week, fueling rumors, which persist to this day, that it was faked. His legacy lives on, in one way or another. (Michael Ochs)

this page: (b. 1/22/60, # MICHAEL HUTCHENCE

Sydney, Australia, d. 11/22/97) A teen Hutchence, the son of a garment worker father and makeup artist mother, was a skilled swimmer and loved to ride bikes; as an adult, he kept his athletic physique and crossed the oceans to become an international star. In the late seventies, Hutchence joined with a school friend, Andrew Farris, and formed the group, The Farris Brothers. The first day they performed together was August 16, 1977—the day Elvis Presley died. In 1980, they changed their name to INXS, and set about climbing the Australian music charts. They fared only moderately well for the first few years; it was not until "Original Sin" in 1985 that they reached the summit. The single also drew attention from overseas, and the band gathered raves for their elegant blend of rock, soul, and dance. Slim-hipped Hutchence—in his gaucho-inspired outfits—was being compared to Mick Jagger and Jim Morrison. Their best year began late in 1987, with the release of the superbly stylish and sexy worldwide number-one "Need You Tonight"—accompanied by an equally innovative video. But Hutchence was a troubled soul who found it hard to cope with fleeting fame. Although his career was far from over and he gave no warning signs, recent recording inactivity and troublesome personal relationships took their toll. He took his own life by hanging himself with a belt in a Sydney hotel room. (Neal Preston/Corbis)

BOBBY Darin

opposite: (b. Walden Robert Casotto, 5/14/36, New York City, d. 12/20/73) Singing professionally since the mid-fifties, Darin earned a reputation for being brash and cocky, once comparing himself (quite unabashedly) to Frank Sinatra and memorably exclaiming that he expected to be a legend by the time he was twenty-five. Such hubris was not without its reasons: when Darin was a child, rheumatic fever damaged his heart and doctors felt he would not live long. Knowing this made it doubly important for him to become a success in show business—and fast! The novelty song "Splish Splash" (1958) and the splendid pop ballad "Dream Lover" (1959) were two early hits (which he also composed), but they bore little resemblance to the type of music for which he is most remembered. Late in 1959, Darin made an abrupt career change by turning directly to the adult market. A gamble for any teen idol, it paid off for Darin. Showing adeptness at nightclub-style entertainment, he released "Mack the Knife" (from the 1928 score of *The Threepenny Opera*), which was a landmark event. For a then-twenty-four-year-old Darin, its popularity—nine weeks at number-one and Grammy for Record of the Year—bridged the generation gap and indeed made him legendary. However, for the rest of his life, Darin endured more than his share of ups and downs. His 1960 marriage to teen-queen Sandra Dee ended after years of tension and hostility in 1967. At age thirty-two, he learned that his older sister was actually his mother (he had been raised by his grandmother to prevent scandal). Darin was also an acclaimed actor, receiving an Academy Award nomination for *Captain Newman, MD* (1963) but appeared in only a handful of films. Disillusioned with his work in general he became involved in the late sixties civil rights movement and recorded folk music ("If I Were a Carpenter," 1967). Unfortunately, his fans did not follow. Finally, in the early seventies, he sought to reinvigorate his career with a television variety show, but it lasted only one season. Soon after, Darin lost the battle with his own fragile body. (Michael Ochs)

this page: (b. Charles Hardin Holley, 9/7/36, Lubbock, Tex, d. 2/3/59) He learned to play the fiddle and piano as a child, but as Holly grew older he gravitated to the guitar. As a talented teen—he wrote all his own material—Holly was signed to Decca Records. But it proved a false start; not yet ready, he returned to Texas. Back on native soil, he formed the band The Crickets (whose unique "black" sound got them booked into Harlem's famed Apollo Theater). With "Peggy Sue" and "That'll Be the Day," they were on the fast track to fame and fortune, but Holly broke away from the group and moved to New York's Greenwich Village. There, he married Maria Elena Santiago and started a family. Then in early 1959, Holly set off on a tour of the midwest. The plane crash that took his life and that of Ritchie Valens and the Big Bopper also caused his wife to miscarry. (The Don McLean hit "American Pie" was named for the plane carrying Holly, and the lyric "the day the music died" was attributed to refer to the fallen singer.) Holly, in his trademark bookish wide-rimmed glasses and distinctive "hiccup" vocal style, became an unlikely teen idol—he lacked the same obvious sexual appeal of an Elvis Presley—but because of his brief, acclaimed career, he was guaranteed the status of a legend. (Michael Ochs)

Kurt Cobain

opposite: (b. 2/20/67, Aberdeen, Wash., d. 4/5/94) As a troublesome youngster, Cobain was given Ritalin to help him concentrate in school and sedatives to help him sleep. Then he was sent to live with relatives. His unruly behavior was defused by painting and singing; he bought his first guitar at age fourteen. With only a few weeks left until graduation, he dropped out of high school. Unable to hold down a job, he formed Nirvana in 1986, but it would be years before they made their historic impact. After releasing *Bleach* in 1989—to no fanfare—they returned with *Nevermind* (1991) and were thrust into the forefront of the music scene. As the blond, blue-eyed lead singer and guitarist of the band, Cobain became grunge rock's reluctant poster boy, but he vehemently disliked the attention. In particular, he preferred playing intimate venues to the large arenas in which they were suddenly thrust. But his dislikes were placated by the tubs of money he earned and the drugs—heroin and morphine—that the cash could buy. In 1992, his dark life brightened somewhat when he married Courtney Love and had a daughter, Frances Bean. But by the next year he overdosed and sought rehab. That same year, 1993, the group released its last album, *in utero*. Early the following year, they played a concert in Munich. A week later, Cobain was hospitalized in a coma. Upon waking, he left voluntarily, then disappeared, and was found three days later in his Seattle home, dead of a gunshot wound. (Levy/Retna)

this page: (b. Lesane Parish Brooks, 6/16/71, New York City, d. 9/13/96) Shakur, whose full name comes from the ancient Incan language words for "shining serpent," was with the group Digital Underground until his breakthrough solo release *2Pacalypse Now* in 1991. Instantly becoming a lead figure in in the category of "gangsta" rap—with lyrics often referring to sexual violence and cop killing—he tempered his volatile music career with a credible turn to leading man in film. Nevertheless, neither his professional nor private life was ever far from controversy. Both his mother and father were members of the political group the Black Panthers, but amidst the instability he found safe haven as a teen when his talents allowed him to attend Baltimore's School for Performing Arts. Shakur's only marriage, to Keisha Morris, was annulled, but he was considered one of music's most eligible bachelors and was even engaged to Quincy Jones's daughter Kidada. In 1994, he was jailed for fifteen days on an assault and battery charge, then in 1995 he was convicted of sexual assault and served eight months behind bars. Shakur's shooting death in New York's Times Square sparked the intense, often violent, East Coast–West Coast rap feud and also triggered the killing of fellow rap artist The Notorious BIG. Although ownership of Shakur's estate has been under constant dispute between family members and past associates since his demise, there have been numerous successful releases of "new" material, and the man's status among urban music enthusiasts continues to flourish. (Gerber/Corbis)

TUPAC SHAKUR

Marvin Gaye

(b. Marvin Pentz Gay Jr., 4/2/39, Washington, D.C., d. 4/1/84) Here was the "lover man" of soul music. Named after his father, a minister, Gaye first sang with the church choir at age three until leaving to join the group The Rainbows. By 1961, he had moved to Detroit and signed with Motown. That same year he married founder Berry Gordy's daughter, Anna. Early success came with smooth and romantic R&B dance hits. By the mid-sixties, his songs became more sophisticated, and with "Ain't That Peculiar" he became the label's best-selling male artist. Gaye was the consummate "ladies man," and recorded a number of upbeat, romantic duets with Tammi Terrell that represent the best of their type, while continuing his solo recording (including Motown's then-best-selling single "I Heard It through the Grapevine"—a year before Gladys Knight's version). When Terrell died in 1970 (the result of a brain tumor), Gaye was devastated. He rose from the loss of a good friend and collaborator but found his next work at first refused by Motown. The album, *What's Goin' On*, musically highlighted the plights of then-contemporary urban culture and is now considered one of the greatest of all R&B recordings. Ironically, the work that followed was a major spiritual reversal. Focusing on his personal life and sexuality, he released the highly erotic album *Let's Get It On*, containing the sublime hit disco party song "Got to Give It Up." But by then, in real life, he was "giving up" a lot. Gaye unamicably broke up with Anna (but married again); developed a serious cocaine habit; had enormous tax problems; had an irreconcilable dispute with Motown; and then moved to Europe. He reemerged in 1982, with a new label, Columbia, and the hit "Sexual Healing." Unfortunately, his continuing dependency on drugs fueled a long-standing dispute with his father, with whom he was now living. During one rather explosive encounter, Sr. Gaye, acting in self-defense, shot his son dead. Gaye's legacy is a journey through all of contemporary black music: from doo-wop to slick soul pop, political anthems to sensuous dance music—and a bittersweet mix of pleasure and pain. (Michael Ochs)

sam cooke

(b. Sam Cook, 1/22/31, Clarksdale, Miss., d. 12/11/64) He was considered the first "superstar" of soul, also had a reverend for a father, and, as a youngster, sang with his three siblings under the name The Singing Children. As he matured, Cooke sang with gospel groups. But when he first recorded secular music, it was under the pseudonym "Dale Cook" so as not to offend religious fans. His seminal "You Send Me" was surprisingly disliked by his first record label, and he was released from his contract. Moving on to another label, Keene, he and the song became smash hits. But further label discontent led Cooke to RCA, where he released his own compositions "Chain Gang" and "Cupid," among others. With a naturally spectacular singing voice, dashing good looks, and a marvelous sense of style, his career was in full swing when multiple tragedy struck. In 1963, his wife died in a car accident and one of his sons (of six children) drowned. In 1964, in an altercation involving a woman whom Cooke had apparently picked up, he was shot dead by a female motel owner—although details surrounding his death remain highly mysterious. Released posthumously, Cooke's song "Change Is Gonna Come" presaged the coming struggle of domestic racism and kept the man's work at the forefront of soul music, even after his death. (Wallace Seawell/MPTV)

Prince (b. Prince Roger Nelson, 6/7/58, Minneapolis, Minn.) This diminutive devil (five-foot-two) was named after the group The Prince Roger Trio, for whom his father was a singer. At age seven, his parents divorced, and living with dad, he received his first guitar. Immediately, Prince showed amazing skill with musical instruments and songwriting. With a friend Andre Anderson (later Andre Cymone) he formed a band, and by high school—under the name Champagne—they were playing Prince-penned compositions. By the time he wrote "When Doves Cry" in 1984 (from the Oscar-winning soundtrack for *Purple Rain*) he had complete control over all aspects of his work—relatively unheard of for one still so young—and had created a not-so-quiet revolution with his blatant onstage sexual antics and offstage sexual ambiguity. Astoundingly prolific, his career has been filled to overflowing with toe-tapping gems, amidst the occasional sinking stone, and has also helped other acts by producing and furnishing hit songs, including The Bangles ("Walk like an Egyptian"), Sinead O'Connor ("Nothing Compares 2 U"), Sheila E. ("The Glamorous Life"), and Sheena Easton ("Sugar Walls"). Sometimes, as with the latter piece, Prince's lyrics could be so controversial the songs were banned from radio airplay in many places. Unfortunately, a long festering quarrel with his record company, Warner Bros., over releaseable material resulted in his name change to an infamously unpronounceable symbol. A short time later, he allowed himself to be called "the artist formerly known as Prince," but it did little to help his career, which at that time was in decline. But the phrase became an instant classic! He has since reverted back to Prince. (Michael Ochs)

BiLLY iDOL

b. William Michael Albert Broad, 1/30/55, Stanmore, Middlesex, England) Idol took his name from a remark made by a schoolteacher who said that he was "idle" in school (he also dropped out of college after only one semester). In 1976, he formed the punk group Chelsea, but they quickly folded. Idol then created Generation X, which lasted only until 1981, when he went solo. Though forever associated with the British music scene and their revolutionary punk rockers (Sid Vicious, et al.), Idol began the more successful part of his career in America, with the release of a self-titled debut album and the hits "White Wedding" and "Hot in the City." Shirtless and tattooed, bound tightly in leather pants, with spiky white-blond hair, icy-blue eyes, and a forced sneer, Idol played the part of rock bad-boy to the hilt and benefited greatly in the new "video" milieu by virtue of his undeniable sexual energy. In 1993, he had a near fatal motorcycle accident. He has long since fully recovered, but his life continues to be one wild ride. Yet despite his nonconformist ways—he claims to have inherited his rebellious streak from his father and grandfather—Idol found much more commercial success and longevity than his contemporaries. (Corbis)

HENRY ROLLINS

(b. Henry Garfield, 2/13/61, Washington, D.C.) Rollins—if you can believe it!—once worked as a manager in a Haagen-Dazs ice cream shop. (One scoop or two, dude?) So heavily muscled, sweaty, and tattooed, Rollins has looks that could get him mistaken for a bouncer or even better, a professional wrestler, but unlike those ringside behemoths, he is intensely earnest—at times humorous—and unflaggingly focused on his unusual music career (although he has added part-time "acting" to his workload). He became the vocal lead for the notorious band Black Flag (considered one of the "roughest" groups in music history), after jumping onstage one night and wresting the microphone away to perform a song. As a member, he lived for years in a van before striking out on his own with The Rollins Band. His spoken word recordings (including *Get in the Van: On the Road with Black Flag,* which won a 1994 Grammy) have made him something of a modern-day prophet to his ardent fans. Surprisingly, none of them are put off by his political-correctness, especially when espousing his views on intolerance of racism and acceptance of all sexual orientations. For all his bicep-bulging bravado, Rollins is quite uncomfortable with his notoriety. He attributes this dislike of public attention to harsh parts of his life that he had to endure privately: a childhood of abuse at the hands of his father and the witnessing of a best friend's murder during a botched robbery attempt. (Eddie Malluk/Retna)

(b. 11/1/62, Grand Rapids, Mich.) Kiedis's group The Red Hot Chili Peppers began as a garage band named Anthem, eventually earning a formidable reputation for their live performances. Their act was often peppered with risque moments, such as appearances onstage wearing nothing but striped white sweatsocks pulled over their genitalia, and constant "playful" harassment of female fans. The two original members, Kiedis and Balzary, met while in a Los Angeles high school. Early on, frequent lineup changes made it hard for the band to find a consistent sound and commercial success, until their breakthrough album, *Blood Sugar Sex Magik*, was released in 1991. Intermittently, members, including Kiedis, have fought substance abuse (one founding member, Hillel Slovak, died of a heroin overdose) but have overcome the obstacles to become one of the most liked and praised alternative rock bands in decades. A hopeful sign of the times: they sustained their popularity while unapologetically homoeroticizing part of their public persona. A perfect example: the great video screen kiss between Kiedis and onetime drummer, heartthrob Dave Navarro. (Larry Busacca/Retna)

anthony kiedis

Fred Durst

(b. William Frederick Durst, 8/20/70, Gastonia, N.C.) He was the son of a policeman and moved to Jacksonville in his teens. A self-professed "freak," Durst was not a good student in school (no!) and ended up serving a stint in the navy, got married at age twenty (had a daughter), and divorced his wife when he discovered she was cheating. He then spent a short time in jail for assaulting her "lover." Durst also became an avid skateboarder before forming his hard rock, hip-hop—sometimes going under the label "nu metal"—band, Limp Bizkit, in 1994. Stockily built and nearly bald, with a jawline-sharpening soul patch, wearing his prerequisite backward-turned baseball cap and oversized jersey top, Durst has become an instantly recognizable, astonishingly sexy (even rather sweet-looking) visual icon of twenty-first century rock music. Admittedly a touch self-important, this onetime professional tattoo artist (who still practices the craft today) will diss pop diva Christina Aguilera, while at the same time rerecord gay-cult classics like "Relax Go to It," without batting a blue-eye. Is somethin' up here, guys?! A telling quote: "It's good to be a rock star; you get into restaurants dressed like crap when you're supposed to have a suit on." (Bob Mussell/Retna)

(b. James Todd Smith, 1/14/68, St. Albans, Queens, N.Y.) LL Cool J—whose name is an acronym for "ladies love cool James"—began rapping at age nine; by sixteen, beefy and bare-chested, sporting audaciously large gold chains, a Kangol hat, and baggy Adidas sweats, he was a major star. As the unofficial "lady-killer" of pop music's most urban sound, LL's macho persona is disarmingly tempered with charm and humor, but his work has not been without controversy. Though the lyrical rhetoric, of songs like "Mama Said Knock You Out," is far less vitriolic than that of his peers, the occasional public appearance has met with untoward moments (although the rapper's personal involvement has been incidental). However, his crossover-to-pop success has provoked cries of "sellout" from some critics. The first artist to record with the legendary label Def Jam, LL has a passion for music that was influenced early in his life by his grandfather's love of jazz and the performers on television's *Soul Train*. Today, considered one of rap's "senior" players, he has quite ably taken his buff physique into television and film acting. (Janette Beckman/Retna)

AXL rose

opposite: (William Bailey, 2/6/62, Lafayette, Ind.) Years before founding the controversial rock band Guns 'N Roses, little Axl (the name taken from an earlier group) began singing, at age five, in his church choir (yep, I said church!). Sadly, Rose's childhood was far from angelic. Filled with abuse from his father and stepfather, it no doubt influenced his often irrational and sexist adult behavior, homophobia (although he did appear at Freddy Mercury's AIDS benefit concert), and racism. Regardless, with an enormous and solid fan base of "like-minded" straight white males, Rose (which was his father's last name) and his band became enormously successful— for a time, even dominating the pop charts—before their public (and private) lifestyle, consisting of too much alcohol, drugs, obscenity, and disorderly conduct, became too much for *anyone* to handle. For a time though, running around onstage in a pair of tight red, white, and blue spandex shorts (so patriotic!)—emphasizing his privates in public—Rose reveled in his prominent (frequently protruding!) role as one of rock's most formidable sex symbols. Surprisingly, flaunting himself near-naked onstage made him increasingly popular with women, but he never lost the cultlike adoration of his male audience (hmmmm?!). That is, until the advent of the slightly mellower, infinitely more introspective musicians of grunge rock knocked him and his band out of the ring. (Neal Preston/Corbis)

this page: (b. Marshall Bruce Mathers III, 10/17/73, Kansas City, Mo.) For many, to have included Eminem within the pages of this book is heresy (on the flip side, I do not expect that Mr. Mathers, given its context, would appreciate being included either). But, to paraphrase Culture Club's Boy George (who is, notably, *not* included herein), "You can hate what a man stands for and still want to sleep with him." Alright, so he isn't exactly a ripped Adonis, but "Slim Shady" has taken average good looks and made himself seem doubly attractive (literally and figuratively) by using the ultimate bad boy stance: refusal to apologize or take responsibility for the serious implications of his actions. His entire career is a sound argument that any publicity, good or bad, can make you popular. While one cannot help but be greatly troubled by the blatantly homophobic, sexist, and violent lyrics of his "music," for the time being the personal and public controversy that continues to swell around him (he recently divorced his wife, retaining shared custody of their little girl, and is still in legal dispute with his own mother, who claims libel and slander against her son) reflects an even larger dilemma. If an artist's work, regardless of content recorded under the guise of free speech, sells in vast quantities, then business (and the public) will turn a deaf ear to the arguments against it. (Kelly A. Swift/Retna)

eminem

snow

(b. Darrin O'Brien, 10/10/69, Toronto, Canada) The precarious nature of "pop" stardom is such that you can have one of the most popular songs of the year ("Informer," 1993) but virtually see yourself disappear by the next. This may be the simple explanation for the career of O'Brien, who, going under the moniker Snow, found himself on top of the music world with the best-selling reggae single, ever, and the distinction of becoming the then most commercially successful white disc jockey—before tumbling out of sight literally overnight. But there is always more to the story. Raised poor in the projects of Toronto (yes, it has projects!), O'Brien spent his teens listening to Kiss. By hanging out with Jamaican residents, he became adept at their *patois* (the local derivation of their native language), and the sound obviously influenced his own music. Despite the owlish spectacles and boy-next-door looks, young O'Brien was also said to have a short-fused temper. Dropping out of school in the eighth grade, he landed in jail twice; the first go-round, for eighteen months, was on a murder charge he was eventually acquitted of. The experience inspired his hit. Nevertheless, during his second incarceration, on a far lesser charge stemming from drinking (another bad habit he developed), O'Brien was behind bars while the song rose up the charts. Talk about awful timing! His debut record was not-too-subtly titled *12 Inches of Snow*, but for all the brouhaha it came up rather short in terms of additionally commercial material. O'Brien continues to record and dj today, but has found it difficult to repeat earlier success. The forecast? Little to no significant amounts of snowfall in the near future. (Michael Benabib/Retna)

vanilla ice

(b. Robert Matthew Van Winkle, 10/31/67, Miami Lakes, Fla.) Ice was raised by his mother and car dealer stepfather (he never knew his real father) and despite attempts to the contrary seems to have had a nicer than grim childhood. Yes, he did hang out in the streets (but what kid didn't at least once?!) and was knifed just one time (not the five times he claimed)—and on his buttocks! For goodness sake, he sang in the church choir until he was fifteen! Clearly, fraudulent details seemed necessary to "legitimize" this pretty white boy's foray into an angry black male-dominated field. Maybe he was too handsome; he was one of *People* magazine's 50 Most Beautiful People in 1991. His face, at least at the start, helped his career. The group Public Enemy encouraged their label to sign the good-looking young man with the breakdance routines. Under his management, the "Iceman" was copied after rapper MC Hammer—especially in costume and choreography—but he himself had more serious intentions for his future. Nevertheless, to quickly cash in on his teen idol popularity, the six-foot-three icicle was rushed into the film *Cool as Ice*. By the time of its release, his career was even colder than that. Ice also gamely appeared in Madonna's book *Sex*. Though he often claimed to be rather substantially endowed, you'll find no evidence therein. He still performs today—a little older, wiser, and arguably, even better looking. (Neal Preston/Corbis)

135

mick jagger

(b. Michael Phillip Jagger, 7/26/43, Dartford, Kent, England)) An alarmingly thin, rubbery-faced, longlimbed, and ofttimes unabashedly androgynous man, Jagger was a most improbable rock sex symbol, but become one he did. Taking what to others may have been perceived as physical shortcomings, he turned them to his benefit; and all the men this side of "buff and beautiful" owe him a great debt. Jagger showed that women could fall for a guy who was oddly appealing and aggressively sexual—and not necessarily a hundred percent heterosexual. A shy, middle-classed student of economics, he discontinued his studies to become the best known "front man" in music—for the band The Rolling Stones (the name came from the lyrics to a Muddy Waters song). Purposely, Jagger has stayed away from solo outings—only now having released his fourth individual recording (to a surprisingly small amount of fanfare in his native country)—which kept the integrity of the act intact for nearly four decades. But his personal life was not nearly as consistent or considerate. While the Stones became more successful and influential, this devilish dervish embraced the darker side of fame and fortune and became enmeshed in wanton (hetero-, homo-, and bi-) sexual behavior, drugs, and alcohol. So excessive was this chapter in his life—from the sixties into the seventies—that he doesn't sufficiently remember enough details to pen an accurate biography. Now a father of seven, grandfather, and ex-husband to Bianca Morena and Jerry Hall, Jagger has calmed down considerably as he nears his sixtieth birthday. (Neal Preston/Corbis)

rod stewart

(b. Roderick David Stewart, 1/10/45, London, England) Stewart was a gifted English football (soccer) player, but dropped the ball to become the most popular British singing star of the seventies. (Soccer is still his second love after music.) Also a talented harmonica player, Stewart started in the sixties with a folk band, then an R&B group, before attracting attention when he joined The Jeff Beck Group in 1966. Earning the nickname "Rod the Mod," this five-foot-five singer quickly became known for his frail and hoarse voice, dandy duds, and randy behavior. Over the years, his relationships with famous women, including Britt Ekland, Alana Hamilton, Kelly Emberg, and Rachel Hunter, have received almost as much attention as his work. During the early seventies, as he began to record solo, he introduced in his orchestrations the mandolin (thanks to player Martin Quittenton). The resulting sound made his records, in particular "Maggie May," instantly distinctive—and massive hits. Strutting around onstage with his stick-straight straw blond hair, pink satin jumpers, and the occasional touch of powder eye shadow, he came across wittier and more wiley than your average rocker. Over the decades, Stewart has been able to successfully incorporate almost every genre of music into his career—including disco on his biggest hit "D'Ya Think I'm Sexy" (the royalties of which he gives to charity because he doesn't actually like the song and how the lyrics have been interpreted). Stewart has also never won a competitive Grammy, having been nominated only once (for "Downtown Train") and has been criticized as often as he collects gold records. I guess "some guys have all the luck"—and some don't. (Lynn Goldsmith/Corbis)

roger DALTREY

(b. 3/1/44, London, England) Daltrey is an academically brilliant and self-proclaimed anti-everything person, but he has never felt less than positive about becoming a rock star; but prior to forming his first band, The Detours, in 1963, he was a sheet metal factory worker. He is considered combative and pugnacious—which some say stems from his relative short stature (five-foot-six)—and being in his company can be rather dangerous. He has been known to throw punches at fellow bandmates and bystanders. But he quickly learned to transfer his anger and frustration into a memorable stage personality, one that conveys pathos and bewilderment to much audience ardor. In 1964, his group made the fateful decision to change their name to The Who, and live rock music itself was never quite the same experience. With Daltrey as the driving force and man-of-action, and Pete Townsend as the idea-and-experiment person, the group offered up their highly innovative, 1969 masterwork *Tommy*—giving the world its first rockopera. As the gold-and-curly haired, bare-chested, blind protagonist in the piece, a sinewy Daltrey became the archetype male rock star and sex symbol (it didn't hurt matters that he was exceedingly proud of his perfectly tight little body, and took every opportunity to show it off). By the time he recreated his "role" in the 1975 film version, Daltrey was already spending more time on acting and solo recording efforts (though the latter has not reaped substantial commercial rewards). The Who officially broke up in 1982 but has reunited for a number of special occasions. On the personal side, Daltrey has stayed married to wife Heather Taylor for more than thirty years—something quite unique in the world of entertainment—and they have five children. (Michael Ochs)

PETER FRAMPTON

(b. 4/22/50, Beckenham, Kent, England) As a seven-year-old, this gangly young lad was obsessed with his grandmother's *banjolele* (a banjo-shaped ukelele) and taught himself how to play it before turning to the guitar and songwriting a year later. Growing up to become an absolutely adorable "mod" London teen, talented Frampton—then appearing with an act called The Herd—was named by the British press as the "Face of 1968." Then, in 1969, as a member of the group Humble Pie, he grew his hair long and set out to become a rock star. He released *Frampton Comes Alive* in 1975, which sold a phenomenal twelve million copies, becoming the biggest-selling "live" album in history. This amazing and early feat still puzzles some rock critics, who considered the work nothing more than a very good effort. Incidentally, acclaimed film director Cameron Crowe wrote the original liner notes on *Frampton Comes Alive*; in turn Frampton was "authenticity advisor" on Crowe's semibiographical picture *Almost Famous* (2000). Even more puzzling at the time, Frampton's recordings were not as popular in his native England, and the follow-up album, *I'm in You*, was deemed a failure because it sold *only* three million copies. In 1978, he made the questionable decision to appear in Robert Stigwood's film *Sgt. Pepper's Lonely Hearts Club Band*, along with the BeeGees—alas neither one's fans followed them into the theater. It was the only feature film either would ever make. Upon his return to recording shortly thereafter, Frampton found that fans had not followed him back to record stores either. Not until many years later, with the 1995 release of *Frampton Comes Alive II* was he able to reinvigorate his stalled music career. (Lynn Goldsmith/Corbis)

139

THE GUYZ

JOHN SEBASTIAN

(b. 3/17/44, New York City) Not since Buddy Holly had a guy in glasses elicited such ardor from fans. Sebastian was brought up in the heart of New York City by his classical harmonica-playing father (yes, there was a time when you could get a job playing the harmonica!) and writer-mother, who both nurtured Sebastian's musical calling. As a student of New York University, he frequented the Greenwich Village haunts where innovative musicians played into the wee small hours. When Sebastian joined his first band, its membership included singer Maria Muldaur ("Midnight at the Oasis"); his second contained Cass Elliott (pre-Mamas and Papas). As the founding member and lead songwriter of the group, Lovin' Spoonful, he and his band mates proved that all was not lost to the mid-sixties "beat" wave from England. Teenaged fans partied hard to their hits "Do You Believe in Magic" and "Summer in the City"—all composed by Sebastian—making their music the perfect background sounds for the ever-unifying youth culture of America. However in 1968, the band dismantled—the year the youth movement crested. (The group reformed, but without Sebastian.) On his own, this hirsute little hunk made a go at a solo career with varying degrees of success. He performed to much acclaim at the legendary Woodstock concert in 1969, and initial albums were critical successes. However, a live appearance on *Saturday Night Live* to sing his surprise hit theme from television's *Welcome Back, Kotter* was met with a harsh audience reception. It seemed that in the year 1976 youthful optimism had quickly been replaced by mature cynicism. (Henry Diltz/Corbis)

James Taylor

(b. 3/2/48, Boston, Mass.) A child of wealth, who was encouraged to pursue music, Taylor would want for nothing it appeared. But like many of his generation, he still chose to rebel against the establishment and his family. Handsome Taylor's situation was unique. He suffered from severe mental depression and for a time had to be institutionalized. Seemingly cured, he moved to New York City, whereupon he was beset upon by the usual hangers-on, who found Taylor and his money too attractive to resist. Thanks to his often unsavory companions, he fell into more mental instability and developed a dangerous drug addiction. Fortunately, Taylor was able to fend off the "monkey on his back"—aided by his burgeoning musical talents. When he wrote "Fire and Rain" (1971) it was as much an autobiographical composition as it was deemed a paean to the close of the psychedelic sixties. During this next decade, Taylor became immensely popular as a foxy folk/pop artist who bridged the two generations with touching tunes like "You've Got a Friend." For a time he was married to singer Carly Simon. Considered the "golden union" of its day, the marriage ended in the early eighties. However, Taylor continues to be a "friend" to her—and to all of us. (Henry Diltz/Corbis)

Bryan Adams

(b. 11/5/59, Kingston, Ontario, Canada) Unbeknownst to many, even some of his most devoted fans, Adams recorded the disco-lite hit "Let Me Take You Dancing" in 1979. Give it a listen if you can! Adams's father was a diplomat, so as a youth he was educated around the world. When he was sixteen, he was given a piano and began to write music. As Canada's most popular male pop-rock artist export (one guess for the most popular female: Celine Dion), raspy-voiced Adams is much like many from his native country: nonaggressive, while at the same time resolute; full of talent, but without the bravado. For a few years after his onetime "trip" on the dance floor, this sensitive singer spun around until the release of his third album, *Cuts Like a Knife* (1983), found an audience. Ever since, his unique mix of a shy demeanor with an almost pained-sounding vocal style began winning the hearts and minds of soft rock aficionados around the world. In fact, one of his biggest hits—"Everything I Do (I Do It For You)" from the soundtrack to *Prince of Thieves* (1991)—was the longest charting number-one single *ever* in England. (That includes the Beatles.) This release, as well as two others, netted the boyishly cute (and still so now) singer three Oscar nominations, but all failed to win. (Mark Anderson/Retna)

rick springfield

(b. Richard Lewis Springthorpe, 8/23/49, Sydney, Australia) This son of an army officer (who moved a great deal) grew up in England, and it was there that he developed an interest in music. (Springfield got his first guitar from Woolworth's when he was thirteen.) Returning to Australia as a teen, he joined a Melbourne band, playing the piano and guitar. By the late sixties, he had hooked up with another band who, among other venues, performed amidst shelling in war-torn Vietnam. Moving to America in 1972, he was groomed as a music teen idol, but things didn't work out as neatly as originally planned. He had to sign a television contract with Universal—appearing in shows ranging from *The Incredible Hulk* to *The Rockford Files*—to make ends meet. And he did the date routine with all the starlets, including Linda Blair. While continuing his tries at music stardom, he landed the role (for eighteen months) of Dr. Noah Drake on the highly rated daytime soap opera *General Hospital*. His almost instantaneous success helped jumpstart his floundering singing career. Meanwhile at home, he took in a homeless mixed-breed dog, whom he named (Lethal) Ron. His furry friend became the cover subject of Springfield's breakthrough album *Working Class Dog* (1980). So close was the singer to his pet that when Ron died in 1995 in tribute he had a soaring hawk (to signify ascendancy into heaven) tattooed onto his back right shoulder. (Gary Gershoff/Retna)

GLENN FREY

this page: (b. 11/6/48, Detroit, Mich.) Early in his career, this hunky dude worked with at least three bands before heading out west with his girlfriend. For a time, he was roommates with Jackson Browne, and sang professionally for Bob Seger, then J. D. Souther, before joining Linda Ronstadt's backup musicians. With fellow player Don Henley, the two branched off to form what is frequently "honored" as the all-time classic American rock band, The Eagles. By far the sexiest member of the group, Frey was cowriter of many of their best works, including "Take It Easy" (which he cowrote with Browne), "Take It to the Limit," and the immaculate "Hotel California." He also sang lead vocals on many of The Eagle's defining hits—"Lyin' Eyes" and "Heartache Tonight" among them. While a member of the band, Frey wore his hair long (often with a head-band), sporting the occasional pair of aviator sunglasses (the unofficial favorite "rock star" shape), and frequently poured into a pair of tight, faded, and strategically torn bell-bottoms— the very picture of a rockin' (and available for action) California stud. After the group broke up in 1981, Frey found success as a solo artist, but his hair was cut short and he fancied the *Miami Vice* pastel-suit-and-T-shirt look (no small coincidence that he was friends with the show's star, Don Johnson). (Roger Ressmeyer/Corbis)

opposite: (b. Hugh Anthony Cregg II, 7/5/51, New York City) No doubt about it, this dude is *the* "guy's guy" type, which may account for his onetime huge, pre-dominantly white, middle-class male "good ole boy" fan base. If The Eagles are considered the quintessential seventies rabble rousers, then arguably, Huey's flock, The News (originally named The American Express in Marin County, California, 1979), was the eighties party group of choice. Playing their soft version of hard rock, the band had a sound that was the perfect frat-boy beer blast mood enhancer. In his black Ray-Ban sunglasses (the eighties shade of choice), skinny tie and suit, lead Lewis became the Pied Piper of up-and-coming yuppies across this great nation. But before all this happened, stud was a high-scoring (test-wise!) Cornell University engineering student who dropped out of academia to traipse across Europe, before landing in San Francisco. There he played music, a habit he picked up abroad, but sustained himself with landscaping and carpentry work. His first professional name was—hold on— "Huey Louie" (named after one of Donald Duck's nephews!), and his first band, for whom he played the harmonica and sang vocals, was called Clover. Luckily, Lewis's success came just in the nick of time: past thirty years of age (*trés* old for a rock star!) he was just about ready to throw in the towel when "Do You Believe in Love" became a hit. The group had eighteen Top 40 placers over the next decade, and three number-ones. Recently, Lewis scored a surprise adult contemporary chart topper with actress Gwyneth Paltrow; the song was a remake of Smokey Robinson's "Cruisin'" and was featured in the 2000 film *Duets,* in which they costarred. (Roger Ressmeyer/Corbis)

Huey Lewis

Jackson Browne

(b. Clyde Jackson Browne, 10/6/48, Heidelberg, Germany) Browne was born in Germany, because father worked there for a military newspaper. In 1951, the family moved to Los Angeles, and as a teen he began writing his own songs. Brown-eyed Browne joined the famous Nitty Gritty Dirt Band in 1966 but lasted with them only six months. He then moved to Greenwich Village (as so many upstart musicians have done over the years) and crossed paths with Andy Warhol. Returning to the west coast in 1968, this beautiful boy wonder was heard by up-and-coming record exec David Geffen, who, in turn, recommended him to music mogul Ahmet Ertegun. Ertegun ventured that if Browne was so talented, why shouldn't Geffen sign him to his own label? So he did. Forming Asylum Records, Geffen signed not only Browne, but The Eagles as well—and the heyday of California rock began. From this auspicious beginning, Browne worked with many of the most influential artists of the day, including Joni Mitchell, Linda Ronstadt, David Crosby, Bonnie Raitt, and The Eagles, and he went on to become one of contemporary music's finest singer/songwriters, with some of the most important rock songs ever written—"Doctor Mine Eyes" and "Running on Empty" as two examples. Also committed to social activism, Browne was responsible for establishing the legendary "No Nukes" concerts. (Michael Ochs)

(b. 10/7/51, Seymour, Ind.) Joining his first band in the fifth grade, Johnnie was thrown off the high school football team for sneaking cigarettes. His eventual five-pack-a-day habit would catch up with his health. When he got a little bit older—and you would hope wiser—a still-teenaged Mellencamp eloped with his pregnant girlfriend. They had the child, but the couple separated in 1975. Shortly after, John moved to New York to start his music career in earnest, while working as a carpenter's assistant to pay bills. Hard to believe, but this roughneck, also tantalizingly described as "hustler-ish," began professionally as a pseudo-glam rock performer. Under the auspices of David Bowie's management, Tony DeVries (and label MainMan), he was positioned as a midwestern James Dean—type—and given the name, Cougar. (He officially began using Mellencamp in 1989.) His first album bombed and he left the label. Mellencamp resented the way he had been handled—a position he has always held against the music industry from the start—and set about making the next time work (and it did). Now being likened to Bruce Springsteen, he clicked. Also similar to "The Boss," Mellencamp's music spotlit the American scene, and early hits from 1982, "Hurts So Good" (a Grammy winner) and "Jack and Diane" (his sole number-one), solidly appealed to working-class music buyers. He has since gone on to become one of music's most successful, though underappreciated, artists. *Billboard* magazine made up for that by awarding him (one of only ten recipients) their Century Award—"for an artist who has not received the recognition his (or her) work deserves." Still a wildcat, "Cougar" is married to onetime supermodel Elaine Irwin, and resides much of the time in his home state. (Corbis)

JOHN MELLENCAMP

(b. John Francis Bongiovi Jr., 3/2/62, Perth Amboy, N.J.) Jon Bon Jovi is about as handsome as they come, and his group, Bon Jovi, was one of the most successful rock acts of the eighties and nineties (alongside the harder-edged act Guns 'N Roses). He got his first guitar from his mother when he was just seven, and performed with no less than five bands before hitting pay dirt with drummer Nico Torres (another band hottie) and the rest of the boys. In a rare move, label execs formed teen focus groups and played for them a selection of the group's songs. Based upon a compiling of favorites, the album *Slippery When Wet* was released. It slammed the competition and sold in record numbers. Complete with curly long hair (the group was known initially as a "hair metal" band), tight leather, sometimes satin stretch pants (what were these men thinking?!), and ripped shirts, Jon quickly became voted "the sexiest" or "most beautiful" rock star. Thankfully, right about the same time he started to devote time to acting during the early nineties, his "scruffy rocker" gave way to his current "leading man" look—far more effectively utilizing his natural attractions. Though he continues to record music, Jonny-boy has become a movie star and was, at press time, set to play a semiregular on television's *Ally McBeal*. (Gavin Evans/Retna)

Bruce Springsteen

(b. 9/23/49, Freehold, N.J.) Bruce is, by many accounts, considered rock 'n roll's greatest living star. Back in 1974, *Rolling Stone* magazine declared him the "future" of the genre. The critic who wrote the piece was so impressed by Springsteen's talent that he quit his job to become his manager. He legitimized the hype with his landmark release *Born to Run* (1975). Already having worked with several other groups prior, he and his illustrious cohorts, The E Street Band, were thrust into music's front ranks—and Bruce, no less, appeared on the cover of *Time*. Unfortunately, for the next several years his work was muffled by management over legal issues. He resurfaced in the early eighties, stronger than before, with the patriotic *Born in the USA* (1982). It became his best-selling album, and "The Boss" found himself a reluctant object of desire. Broodingly sexy and newly buff, this onetime skinny lad was now a certifiable hunk. With biceps and chest bursting out of his rolled-sleeve denim shirt (unbuttoned for emphasis) and tight (rear-enhancing) jeans, he was an obvious turn-on for women, but his attraction with men was no less evident, though a tad more subverted. His popularity was often at odds with the message of his music: humble middle-class values. But the man who once said he learned to play the guitar to "change the world a little bit and meet girls" did just that. Talented Bruce was also responsible for a number of major works by other artists: "Because the Night" (Patti Smith), "Blinded by the Light" (Manfred Mann), and "Fire" (The Pointer Sisters, though it was originally written for Elvis Presley). He also won an Oscar for "Streets of Philadelphia" from the 1994 film *Philadelphia*. (Neal Preston/Corbis)

man 2 man

BONO *opposite:* (b. Paul David Hewson, 5/10/60, Dublin, Ireland) The revered Bono embodies all the best (and sexiest) qualities of music superstardom. Unlike many rough-hewn rockers, he is benevolent, charitable, and unashamedly open-minded (very few musicians of his caliber would chance their status by wearing a dress, which he did in the video for "One"). He is also quite modest about his talent, never pretending to be more than he is. Considering Bono had no musical skills whatsoever when he joined the group (founded by Larry Mullens under the name Feedback, then The Hype, before deciding upon U2 in 1978) and only *after* acceptance did he learn how to sing, it would not be prudent to be too boastful. His voice still retains that strained quality which comes from pushing sound to its limits, and that edge adds to his charisma (the reason, they say, why the talent-lacking youth was hired in the first place). Bono—whose name comes from the Latin meaning "good voice" (even though it was actually derived from Bono Vox, a hearing aid for sale in Ireland!)—and his group have managed to stay relevant far longer than any of their contemporaries. Credit is due to their ability to perform live (a rarity), the timeliness of their music ("I Still Haven't Found What I'm Looking For" has no age), their fearless forays into genres going beyond classic rock (including space age electronica), and, of course, to the inescapable Irish charm of their strutting five-foot-eight, fly-sunglass-wearing leader. (Tony Brady/Retna)

this page: (b. 5/26/64, New York City) Born to a Jewish father (a television producer) and Jamaican mother (the late-actress Roxie Roker, who played Helen on *The Jeffersons*), Kravitz, upon his debut in 1989, immediately drew favorable comparisons to music great Jimi Hendrix for his vintage rock sound and incendiary onstage persona. But this stylish hunk—who was once married to actress Lisa Bonet (of *The Cosby Show*)—has taken his musical celebrity status a step further. By constantly baring his muscular, nipple-pierced chest, occasionally flashing a glimpse of his firm derriere, and changing hairstyles as much as he changes his expensive designer wardrobe, Kravitz projects the image of lusty "plaything" equally with the standard rock male role of "playboy"—making him contemporary rock's sexiest performers in ages. A talented songwriter, Kravitz wrote his own breakout hit "Are You Gonna Go My Way," and Madonna's lusty single "Justify My Love," and has won three Grammys as Best Rock Male Performer. (Lynn Goldsmith/Corbis)

Lenny KraviTz

Harry Connick Jr.

(b. Joseph Harry Connick Fowler Jr., 9/11/67, New Orleans. La.) This cajun cutie's main music repertoire (forties and fifties swing) and manner (smooth and sophisticated) has most often been compared to the professional stylings of Frank Sinatra—not too shabby! (And he sounds a lot like Mel Torme too!) Connick occasionally gets funky and shows his Louisiana roots, even though this tends to dismay some die-hard fans. But it shows that Connick is not just a very good mimic of earlier talents, and he likes to open things up and spread himself around. This multi-Grammy-winning talent began playing the piano at age three, encouraged by his parents, both lawyers, who also owned a record store. Connick shot to prominence on the heels of his soundtrack work for *When Harry Met Sally* (1988). On it he beautifully sang a large selection of classic pop standards. The album became a surprise hit, and so did sharp-suited Connick (often placed on a number of "best-dressed" celebrity lists). (Incidentally, many of Connick's albums are titled by numbers, *11, 20, 25, 30,* which are his age at the time of recording.) Like other handsome and hunky male singers, his good looks carried him over into acting. He has costarred in a number of Hollywood films, including nonsinging roles in *Copycat* (1995) and *Hope Floats* (1998), voiceovers for *The Iron Giant* (1999) and *My Dog Skip* (2000), and the singing part of Lt. Joseph Cable in the television remake of the classic musical *South Pacific* (2001). By late 2001, he had added Broadway composer and lyricist—in *Thou Shalt Not*—to his list of accomplishments. (Bill Davila/Retna)

(b. 6/26/56, Stockton, Calif.) Isaak once had aspirations of being a boxer, but his flattened nose is all that remains of early pugnacious interests. (Smart thinkin, cutie-pie!) He is also a degree-holder in English and, as an exchange student, lived for a time in Japan. It is not so obvious what impression boxing, literature, and Asian culture may have had on his work (maybe something subconscious), but his music was certainly influenced by early fifties rockabilly. Specifically, the "Sun Record" sound—named for the famous Memphis-based blues label that launched Elvis Presley—is one from which Isaak and his backup musicians, at least in the beginning, frequently drew inspiration. Vocally, Isaak was himself frequently likened to legendary singer Roy Orbison. In 1990, after many, many years of trying, Isaak finally landed in the spotlight with his moody hit "Wicked Game," which was featured in the David Lynch film *Wild at Heart*. It also become apparent after watching the Herb Ritts–directed video that the handsome crooner would thereafter have to contend with heartthrob status. Since then, though Isaak has not charted with regularity, his popularity among followers has continued unabated. His quirky celebrity status was even reason enough for him to be given his own cable show, in which this sometime actor stars, not-too-originally titled *The Chris Isaak Show*. The content is based on the idiosyncratic star's real life exploits. (Matt Mendelsohn/Corbis)

(b. 12/9/69, New York City). Dylan has his famous father's curly hair (though cropped much tighter) and intense eyes, but the overall pretty package he likely owes to his ex-model mother, Sara Lowndes. Raised in Los Angeles by mom, after she and dad divorced in 1977, Jakob maintained a good relationship with papa during this time despite the separation, but his life was not as abundantly filled with the sound of music as one would imagine. According to Dylan, music was not just for entertainment, it was for learning—and Dylan Sr. was judicious in his selections. Educated in private schools, young Dylan attended Parsons School in New York as an art student before following destiny's path toward a career in music. To his credit, this sexy young singer never used (or uses) his legendary name to one-up the competition. He formed his group in 1990, under the name Livestock. Surprisingly, given his lineage, their freshman outing failed. Regrouping, with a lineup change and a new esoteric name—The Wallflowers—it clicked. Understandably, the band could not avoid a measure of notoriety for the famous progeny within its midsts. But today Dylan is less prone to avoid the topic, now confident that his own talent is the main attraction. (Neal Preston/Corbis)

(b. 3/15/68, Newport Beach, Calif.) McGrath has multiple tattoos scribbled all over his mean-and-lean body—including the word "Irish" across his back (he is such a good Irish-Catholic boy!)—and used to work as a truck driver before becoming a rock star and sex symbol. Does this information surprise anybody? Just remember that his home-boy habits and pulse-quickening snarls and sneers may be more than just a little exaggerated for those fans out looking for "trouble." After all, he was a communications major at the University of Southern California (USC). College is hardly the route of the true menace to society! He also wears the occasional sleeveless, brightly colored argyle vest while in performance and lavishes attention on his popular "wish-I-had-hair-like-that" haircut—the style of which he deadpans is à la Vanilla Ice. McGrath can also be seen driving the 1968 green Cadillac that was once owned by his grandmother. His group, Sugar Ray, is named for the famed prizefighter and KO'd the competition beginning in 1997 with the six-week number-one "Fly." Since then, fighting off criticism that they are lightweights, the group has had a bit of trouble staying off the mats long enough to top their earlier achievement. Nevertheless, look for McGrath's handsome face to be around for a long, long time. (Astor Morgan/Retna)

mark mcgrath

DON HO

(b. Donald Tai Loy Ho, 8/13/30, Kakaako, Oahu, Hawaii) It's not easy to be considered a rarity in the music business, but certainly this Hawaiian "idol" could be thought of as such. Actually part Hawaiian, Chinese, Portuguese, Dutch, and German, Ho began his career—after serving in the air force—singing at Honey's Cocktail Lounge (named for his mother) on the north side of Oahu. Not a musician beforehand, he learned to play instruments with his hired backup band, The Five Aliis. After outgrowing mama's place, they ventured to beautiful Waikiki Beach in Honolulu and went to work at soon-to-be-famous Duke's. With a drink and cigarette in one hand, while softly playing the organ with the other—Ho took his languid delivery (think of a Hawaiian version of Perry Como) and made the nightclub *the* hottest spot in the Pacific. Locals, tourists, and visitors from around the globe, and many of the biggest stars of the day, came to hear the man (and his band) play a selection of tropical favorites, as well as his memorable "Tiny Bubbles." Soon the world fell under his spell and now, many years later, he has become an indelible part of the culture, officially known simply as "Hawaii's Entertainment Ambassador." (Gunther/MPTV)

HerB ALPerT

(b. 3/3/35, Los Angeles, Calif.) Some listeners stay away from particular music genres based on the perception that because of the category it will not appeal to their tastes. For instance, anything considered "adult music" must be avoided at all costs by any teenager! Certainly much of Alpert's success lies in this much-maligned "easy listening" market. But his music was (and is) sophisticated and sexy—and worth a listen by anyone who can appreciate good music with a good beat. Learning to play the trumpet at age eight, Alpert's prolific career began in the late fifties, when he started arranging, producing, and writing music. He worked with Sam Cooke ("Wonderful World") and Jan and Dean, before founding A&M Records in 1962 with Jerry Moss. Debuting his backup band, The Tijuana Brass, with "The Lonely Bull" (1965), he went on to record "Taste of Honey" (Grammy winner as 1965's Record of the Year), "Spanish Flea," "Casino Royale," and the familiar theme for television's *The Dating Game*. (In 1966, the band's exploits were animated by John Hubley, and the resulting short subject *Herb Alpert and the Tijuana Brass Double Feature* won the Oscar as Best Cartoon.) Despite his good looks, Alpert was uncomfortable with pinup boy status, yet as a reluctant solo singer (who felt he had an unsteady voice) he had a smash hit with Bacharach & David's "This Guy's in Love with You" (1968). In the seventies, his label gave the world The Carpenters; and in 1979 Alpert released his influential, number-one instrumental hit "Rise." Then in 1989, he sold his interest in A&M for an astounding five hundred million dollars! (Gunther/MPTV)

Remember at the end of senior year in high school when names were announced in a number of "best of" categories? Well, in that spirit, an (unscientific and undemocratic) overview of *Boyz* was taken and the happy results follow. So the "winners" are for the "boy" . . .

to take home to mom and marry
Ricky Nelson ("Mystery Date" prize!)

to take to bed as *often* as possible
Enrique Iglesias (is it hot in here?!)

to strip down to his sweat socks
Mark McGrath (the bad-boy next door!)

with a butt like two cantaloupes
Ricky Martin (grab 'em with both hands!)

with arms off of a Greek statue
Tim McGraw (hello, daddy!)

with eyes that twinkle at nite
Michael W. Smith (best seen with lights out!)

with an oh-so-kissable mouth
Harry Connick, Jr. (lip-smackin' good!)

with a bodybuilder chest
Nick Lachey of °98 (he's like Hercules!)

with a *strummable*, 6-pack stomach
Prince (surprised? so was I!)

with sexy, run-your-hands-thru-it hair
Bobby Sherman (it flops in the eyes, too!)

with the most desirable wardrobe
Lenny Kravitz (and a body to match!)

most likely to be a teen idol
Shaun Cassidy (or a kept boy!)

least likely to be a teen idol
Barry Manilow (sorry, girls and boys!)

more like a porn star than a singer
Mark Wahlberg (too obvious?)

CREDITZ

Author's notes: Data used to create the biographical sketches in this book was gathered from a variety of sources, including textbooks, periodicals, video documentation, and, ever-increasingly, internet websites. While the latter proved an abundant source of material, much of what was culled proved inconsistent. Example: stars' ages have a way of changing—you guessed it—to younger dates. Ah, vanity! Forgive me if some of what you read is not the gospel truth; errors are completely unintended. In addition, many of my favorite "hot" men in music (yours too) could not be included for reasons outlined earlier. For one hunk in particular, Paul Parker, a dance music artist ("Right on Target") from the early eighties, I could neither locate a suitable photograph of him nor find sufficient background information. This stuff isn't as easy at it looks! Mr. Parker, if you read this, I am *very* sorry I wasn't able to include you.

The author would like to thank the following individuals and organizations for their help in creating *Boyz and the Bandz:* Chris, my editor, and everyone at Universe; Caroline, my agent; Norman and Donna at Corbis; Yen at MPTV; Helen, Rena, and Jon at Michael Ochs; Christy at Retna; Glenn at Everett; the gents at Photofest; and Globe. He would also like to extend his thanks to the following friends, family, and loved ones for their continued support: Dan and Joe, Tony, Miisa, Lee and family, Mitch and Harris, Joyce, Jim and Gary, Peter and John, Teresa and Ward, Kevin and Alan, Darlene and John, Kevyn and Jeremy, Vicky, Mark, Greg, Dan O., Geoffrey Beene, the Reuters, the Hustons, the Sammons, and, I didn't forget, Red. But most especially the author would like to extend his love and admiration to his partner, Robert, for putting up with all the mess (mental and physical) and for still sticking by his side. XOXO.

rex smith

(b. 9/19/56, Jacksonville, Fla.) With one top-ten, million-selling single—1979's "You Take My Breath Away" from the soundtrack of the TV film *Sooner or Later*—Smith became the last of the seventies teen heartthrobs. Raised in Atlanta, he moved to New York City earlier in the decade and formed a band named—I'll give you a moment to think!—Rex (how original!). However, as a rock star, Smith's appeal was limited. He was too polished and way too pretty for all that rough stuff. With his matinee idol looks and strong voice, he was far better suited to musical theater, which is exactly where his career led. His Broadway debut was as Danny Zuko in the original production of the smash musical *Grease*. After his flirtation with turntable rotation, he went back to The Great White Way to star opposite Linda Ronstadt in *Pirates of Penzance* (he also recreated his role in the film version). For a time, he cohosted the music revue show *Solid Gold* with Marilyn McCoo (in the spot vacated by Andy Gibb), and appeared on the daytime soap *As the World Turns* (1991–93). Nowadays, arguably more handsome and with an even better body that once decorated the back cover of his coveted *Forever, Rex Smith* album, he continues to appear onstage (*The Scarlet Pimpernel*) and records. (Everett)

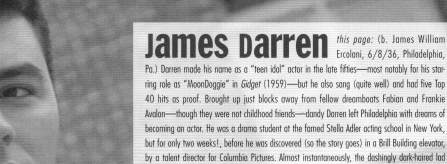

James Darren

this page: (b. James William Ercolani, 6/8/36, Philadelphia, Pa.) Darren made his name as a "teen idol" actor in the late fifties—most notably for his starring role as "MoonDoggie" in *Gidget* (1959)—but he also sang (quite well) and had five Top 40 hits as proof. Brought up just blocks away from fellow dreamboats Fabian and Frankie Avalon—though they were not childhood friends—dandy Darren left Philadelphia with dreams of becoming an actor. He was a drama student at the famed Stella Adler acting school in New York, but for only two weeks!, before he was discovered (so the story goes) in a Brill Building elevator, by a talent director for Columbia Pictures. Almost instantaneously, the dashingly dark-haired lad was signed to a contract. Fast, but not *so* fast, for Darren, who loved to race cars and speed around in motorcycles. Recently, Darren had a "singing" guest star spot on television's *Deep Space Nine*. It proved so popular he joined the cast for an entire season, and went back into the recording studio to cut his first album in over twenty years. In years past, Darren was also a costar on the long-running series, *The Time Tunnel* and *T. J. Hooker*; he is also the father of noted cable TV reporter Jim Moret. (Corbis)

closing page: *NSYNC, on the European CD cover for their number-one single, "Bye, Bye, Bye." (Author's collection)

endpaper: (b. 10/10/54, Bloomington, Ind.) Roth joined a **DaViD Lee RoTH** rock group in 1974, which had the suggestive title Mammoth, but it was soon changed to Van Halen (after founder Eddie's last name). Gene Simmons (of Kiss) discovered the boisterous boys and got them a record deal with Warner Bros. Quickly, "Diamond" Roth became known as the insolent and arrogant bad boy of the group, who fancied the company of strippers, trashing hotel rooms, and making sexist remarks. With his inflated ego, Roth felt he could no longer share the spotlight and quit the band in 1985—to pursue solo recording (with much success) and acting (with relatively none). With all his swagger and overstyled hair, rascally Roth—who loved to "jump" around and bare his hairy haunches for fans (there is *nothing* covering his bottom in this picture!)—turned into a parody of self-love and the excesses of fame, but we loved him just the same! (Neal Preston/Corbis)

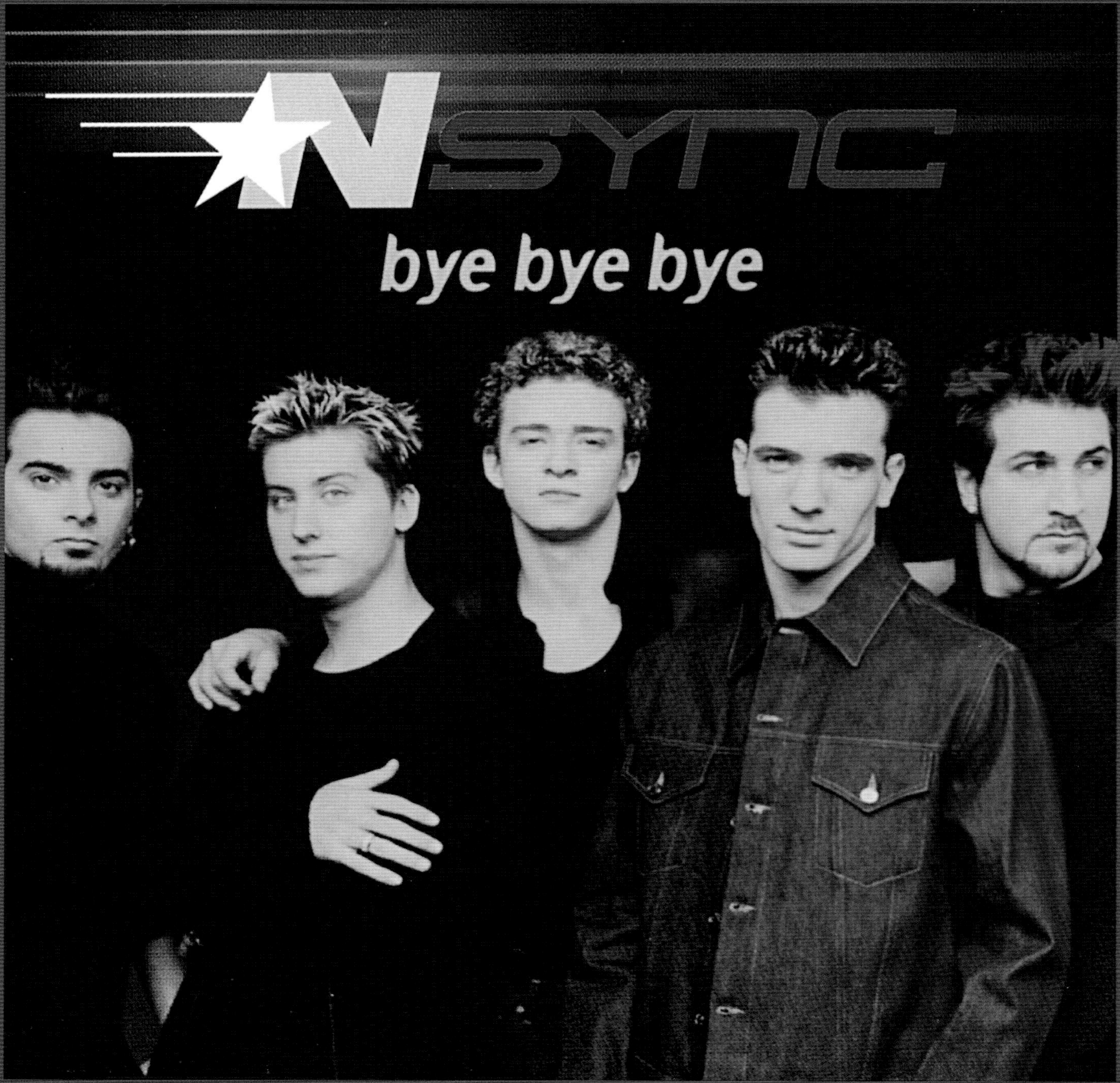
NSYNC
bye bye bye